America Grows Up

AMERICA GROWS UP

A HISTORY FOR PETER

BY
GERALD W. JOHNSON

ILLUSTRATED BY
LEONARD EVERETT FISHER

WILLIAM MORROW AND COMPANY
1960

By the same author

AMERICA IS BORN

Contents

5

CONTENTS

America Grows Up

CHAPTER ONE

The Thirteen Quarrel

IN THE YEAR 1776 on the first day of July nobody denied that the man who was king of England was also king of all the British colonies on the continent of North America. In fact, no one had thought of denying it in all the years since the first British settlement had been established at Jamestown, Virginia, in 1607. But on the fourth day of July, 1776, it was denied, loudly and publicly. On that day delegates sent by thirteen colonies to a meeting in Philadelphia signed a Declaration of Independence, stating that, "These colonies are, and of right ought to be, free and independent states."

It took five years of hard fighting, and two years more of arguing and disputing, to make this statement true, even in part; and it never has been entirely true. Seven years later, in 1783, the British signed a treaty admitting that their king had no more authority over the thirteen colonies. That did make them free and independent of the British Empire, but it did not make them independent of each other.

Wise men knew it, but there never has been a country in which everyone was wise. In 1783 most of the people, if they had been asked about it, would have said that Virginia was no more dependent upon Massachusetts, or Pennsylvania upon North Carolina, than France was upon Spain. The thirteen colonies had fought together against the king, but France and Spain had also fought against him, yet they still remained independent of each other.

To us who are living today the idea that the thirteen colonies could become thirteen independent nations is so silly that we wonder why sane men ever believed such nonsense. But some people did. Most wise men, however, said, "Certainly the thirteen United States are one country." But when it came to acting like one country, nothing was done.

Up to 1776, the people of the different colonies had little contact with each other. If you wanted to go from one colony to another (except for the four small ones in New England) you usually went by ship on the Atlantic Ocean; and once aboard at Charleston or Annapolis, for example, it was about as easy to go east to London as to go north to Boston. Actually it was less dangerous, because sailing along the Atlantic coast through fogs and storms was tricky work.

However, when the Revolutionary War began, the colonies knew they had to stand together, or be beaten one at a time. As far back as 1774, the various colonies had sent men to represent them at a meeting in Philadelphia. Since this congress spoke not for one colony but for all, they called it the Continental Congress. Later the name was changed to the United States in Congress Assembled.

This congress had drawn up a set of rules that every state finally agreed to, although it was 1781 and the war was practically over before the last one, Maryland, came in. These rules were called the Articles of Confederation, and they set up a kind of government for the whole country, but not a very good one. When the peace treaty was signed in 1783, the Americans suddenly discovered that they didn't know what to do next.

It was not so much that nobody had any ideas as that everybody had too many ideas. Some people wanted to make George Washington, who had been Commander in Chief of the American Army, the king of America, but he put a stop to that very quickly. Then some thought we should choose a

French or German prince—nobody wanted an English prince—and make him king. Others were against having a king, but didn't know exactly what they did want. So many people had so many different ideas of what should be done that nothing was done for several years.

In England and other countries of Europe the kings and lords and officers of state looked on at this quarreling and said, "We told you so. The common people can't manage a country. This thing they call the United States of America will soon fall apart and then we can move in and bring them under a king again; if not the king of England, then the king of France, or some other. No country can manage for long without a king."

A great many Americans thought they were right. No country ever had managed without a king. Some had tried it, in times past, but they had always gone back to a king.

There had always been a few people, not only in this country but in Europe before America was discovered, who would not admit that anything had to be so just because it had always been so. These people asked why one man should have the right to give orders that all the others were bound to obey; and they found that the main reason was that the others were afraid not to obey. If they lost their fear, then there would no longer be any reason for a king.

However, it was not true and never had been true that Americans had obeyed the king only because they were afraid not to. That was part of it, but not all. In England for a great many years, for hundreds of years, the people had been growing less and less afraid of the king's soldiers, but more and more afraid of the king's authority. They had been taught to believe that it was very wrong, indeed the worst of crimes, to defy the king. That was what was known as high treason and it was considered worse than the murder of an ordinary man.

Naturally it suited the king to have them believe this, and he did everything he could to persuade the people that it was so. This suited the king's friends, the barons and other lords who shared his power, so they helped him as much as they could. They said that God had chosen one particular man to be king, so to refuse to obey him was to refuse to obey God.

They said all this, and they had been saying it so often and so long that most people believed it. Perhaps it is better to say that they supposed it was so because they never really thought about it. When they did stop to think, they realized that there had been many kings so bad that the people simply couldn't stand them, and either killed them or drove them out of the country. And nothing dreadful had happened to that country.

By 1776, few Americans believed that George III was king by the will of God, or, as people said, by divine right. He was king because the English people were willing to have him, and for no other reason. When the Americans became unwilling to have him any longer, that was the end of it, as far as his rights in America were concerned.

Many Americans had been thinking about this and other problems of government for years and telling other people what they thought. For example, in Massachusetts a man named James Otis and a younger one named John Adams had been making speeches and writing articles, pamphlets, and books about what government is and what it ought to be. In every other colony there were some men doing the same thing, and in Virginia, especially, there were many. People still remember three Virginian Georges — George Mason, George Wythe, and George Washington; three Lees—Richard, Arthur, and Francis; two Randolphs—Edmund, who was for independence, and Peyton, who stuck to the king; and, above all, Thomas Jefferson. All of these men had studied government long and carefully, and could tell other people what they had learned. Then

there was a younger man, not yet famous when the war ended, who was the greatest student in the group. He was James Madison, the best teacher in all Virginia, indeed in all America, of what government ought to be, except for a still younger man in New York, named Alexander Hamilton.

When Jefferson wrote the Declaration of Independence he put a statement in it that referred to the old notion of the divine right of kings. He said that governments "derive their just powers" not from any divine right but from "the consent of the governed." Yet a government of some kind is necessary when people live together, for no one person can do everything that must be done, and someone must say who is to do what. The problem was how to choose the person who was to have the authority.

Americans already had a pattern to follow. Every one of the thirteen colonies had been founded according to some kind of written rules, given by the king and usually called a charter. The charters were quite different, but it was agreed that whatever was the charter was law, not only for the colonists but for the king, too. Neither could change the charter without the consent of the other. More than once the king or the royal governor, who was the king's man in the colony, tried to change or take away a charter, and always there was a tremendous uproar.

In Connecticut once, the governor demanded that the colonists produce the charter, and when it was laid on the table at a meeting it seemed that the governor was about to tear it up or take it away. Suddenly the candles were put out and when they were lighted again the charter was gone. There is a story—nobody knows how true it is—that some colonist snatched up the charter, ran out with it, and hid it in a hollow tree, known from that time on as the Charter Oak. At any rate, Connecticut kept its charter.

Thus when the peace treaty was signed in 1783, Americans were used to the idea that while somebody must be boss, there ought to be limits to what the boss can do, and those limits ought to be written down so that everybody could know what they were. The rules by which a nation is supposed to be run are called a constitution. The charter of each colony had been the constitution of that colony; and when they became independent states most of them simply took the old charter, made a few changes such as striking out all mention of the king of England, and used the rest as the constitution of the state.

The United States in Congress Assembled also had a kind of constitution in the Articles of Confederation, but it was no longer useful. It had been written during the war and its main purpose was to keep the colonies together while they fought Great Britain. Under the Articles all agreed to make war and peace together, to supply money and men to the army, to share the expenses of the central government, and to send men to Congress to make all necessary laws.

The trouble with this agreement was that it didn't bind anybody. If a state decided it did not like a law passed by Congress, it simply refused to enforce that law, and Congress had no power to make the people of that state obey.

The result was a mix-up that very nearly ended all government, and made it hard to do business across a state line. New York and New Jersey fell out over the control of New York harbor, which touched both states. By the terms of its old charter, Maryland owned the Potomac River and refused to let Virginians fish in it, although the south bank of the river was in Virginia. But Virginia owned the capes at the mouth of Chesapeake Bay, which was the only way by which ocean-going ships could come up to Annapolis and Baltimore; so Virginia refused to allow Maryland ships to pass the capes without paying toll. Various states levied special taxes on goods coming in from another state.

Worst of all was the question of money. There never had been gold and silver enough in the colonies to pay for all the goods that were being bought and sold, so people used credit, that is, a promise to pay, instead of gold and silver. Credit has many forms, one of which is paper money.

Now while the war was going on, all the states had issued paper money, and so had Congress. This paper was simply a promise by the state, or by Congress, to pay. But some of the states didn't pay. As for Congress, it had no property it could tax, and no money except what the states agreed to give it. If they went back on their agreement, which some of them did, then Congress had no way of making its paper promises good. So people became less and less inclined to sell their goods for paper money, and the money issued by Congress and some of the states had come pretty close to being worth nothing at all. When people can't buy and sell, business stops; and when they can't buy and sell for anything but silver and gold money, business almost stops, simply because there has never been enough silver and gold to keep trade moving rapidly.

CHAPTER TWO

The Thirteen Become One

BY 1785, two years after the treaty of peace, things were so bad that it was plain to everyone that something had to be done. In that year a committee from Maryland and one from Virginia met at George Washington's home — it was called Mount Vernon, and it still stands on the banks of the Potomac, not far from the city of Washington — to do something about the dispute between Maryland and Virginia over the river and the capes.

They had very little trouble. Quickly and easily they made an arrangement by which Maryland agreed to let Virginians fish in the river provided Virginia would let the Maryland ships pass the capes without paying a toll. It was done so easily that the committee members began to wonder if a meeting of delegates from all the states might not straighten out all the quarrels. It seemed such a good idea that they then and there resolved to ask the state of Virginia to issue a call for a meeting in Annapolis, Maryland, the next year — 1786.

Virginia duly issued the call, but the meeting was a failure. Only five states had delegates there, and five out of thirteen couldn't do anything. However, the meeting was not a total loss, because one of the delegates from New York was Alexander Hamilton, and he was the kind of man who knows how to get things done. Largely through his efforts Congress, not the one state of Virginia, was persuaded to call a third meeting, this one in Philadelphia, in the summer of 1787.

This turned out to be the most important meeting in the history of the United States except the session of the Continental Congress that issued the Declaration of Independence, and in some ways this meeting was even more important than that. It created a new kind of government — a democracy. The word *democracy* is made up of two Greek words, *demos*, meaning *people*, and *kratein*, meaning *to rule*. Thus a democracy is a nation of people who rule themselves — or that is what it is supposed to be.

The idea had been tried before, but it had always broken down because nobody had been clever enough to draw up a set of rules — that is, a constitution — under which it could work. The fifty-five

21

men that the states sent to Philadelphia in 1787 did exactly that, which makes their meeting important not only in American history but in all history, since other nations learned from them.

They began their sessions on May 25, with George Washington presiding, and worked all summer behind closed doors. Newspaper reporters were not allowed to enter and even the members were warned not to keep notes of what was being said. Nevertheless, one of them did, although he did not publish them until many years later; and it is a good thing that James Madison of Virginia broke the rule, because his notes are nearly all that we know about the working of the convention.

This Constitution that they made was a very great charter of government. There is at least one good reason for calling it the greatest ever written. The United States, alone among the great nations, is still governed under its original Constitution after more than a hundred and fifty years. This is proof that it is very good indeed.

Yet at the time there were many people who couldn't see it that way at all. We cannot understand this if we think of the United States as it is today. But in 1787 it was small and poor and weak. The treaty of peace with Great Britain said that the United States should extend from the Atlantic Ocean to the Mississippi River, but it didn't; it extended at most from the ocean to the Appalachian Mountains. To the west of the mountains, there was nothing but forest, except for a few small settlements here and there. Americans were making plans to go into that part of the country, clear the forest, and turn the land into farms, but they had hardly made a start in 1787.

Most of the colonies were vague about their own territory. Virginia, North Carolina, and Georgia were supposed to stretch from the Atlantic to the Mississippi River. Connecticut claimed a great area in what is now Ohio, and Virginia and New York had a sort of title to the rest. But most of the people didn't really care about these claims, because only the land that had people on it was worth owning. And the colonists meant white people, not savage Indians.

The only civilized country was the strip along the Atlantic coast, and that was cut up into thirteen parts. In New England it was not too difficult to get from one colony to another, but once you crossed the Hudson River and started south, you found between the settlements long stretches of wild forest, not a few hundred yards, but miles and miles. In the whole country there was nothing that would now be called a good road. On land, the best way to travel was by horseback, and frequently you could ride a horse all day long without seeing another human being or passing a house.

From a seaport you could travel to another seaport by ship fairly easily; but the ships were driven by wind power, and when the wind was blowing in the wrong direction you simply had to wait until it blew the other way before you could get out of the harbor.

Since it was so hard to get from place to place, the people of one colony didn't see much of the people of any other. They got into ways of thinking and acting that were all their own, so that often a man from Massachusetts simply couldn't understand what made a man from Georgia act as he did; and the Georgian thought that the Massachusetts man had some very queer ideas. The war did more than anything else to make them acquainted with each other. In the army thousands of men traveled more than they had ever done in their lives before and came to know the country much better. But, at that, the various states did not understand each other very well, and so did not trust each other very much.

On one thing, however, the men who came to Philadelphia were agreed. This was that the situation of the country was bad and was getting worse. Many people were sure that Congress could never make its paper money good. Various states were quarreling with each other. In addition to the dispute between Maryland and Virginia and that between New York and New Jersey, most of the states were not allowing goods from other states to come in except by the payment of duties. In short, everybody was trying to take advantage of everybody else. Most people agreed that the basis of the trouble was a bad constitution, and the men who came to Philadelphia had one job only — to improve the Articles of Confederation so that they would work. But these men soon decided that no repair job would make that broken-down machine work again. The only thing to do was to junk it and build a brand-new one with a better design.

So they junked it.

This was a pretty highhanded act, seeing that they had been sent there to repair the old government, not to build a new one. But these were bold men. They knew that what the people needed, and what they really wanted, was a government that would work. No matter what had been said when the convention was called, they made up their minds to give the people what they needed and wanted.

In any case, the people didn't have to take it. One clause in the new Constitution said that each state must call a convention and the convention must

ratify the Constitution before it became law in that
state; and nine of the thirteen states must ratify it
before it became law in any state. That gave the
people a chance to reject the whole thing, if they
didn't like it; and for a while there seemed to be a
good chance that they would reject it.

There were several reasons for this, but the main
one was that the smaller states feared that they
would be gobbled up by the larger ones. If it came
to a fight, Delaware, for instance, would stand no
chance against Pennsylvania, nor Rhode Island
against Connecticut and Massachusetts. It seemed
quite possible that it might come to a fight, for that
had happened more than once in times past. Maryland and Virginia fought a naval war for the possession of Kent Island in the Chesapeake Bay, and the
Virginia Puritans once had invaded and conquered
Catholic Maryland. Just three years earlier the western part of North Carolina had revolted against the
rest of the state and set up what it called the State of
Franklin, and North Carolina was not strong enough
to put down the revolt. In the end this territory,
which had belonged to North Carolina, became the
state of Tennessee.

So the idea that a big state might conquer and
overrun a small one was not as ridiculous as it looks
to us today. As soon as the convention met at Phil-

adelphia, the question of how to protect the small states was brought up. The members looked at it, saw that it was a tough one, and set it aside while they answered some of the others first.

One of the most important questions was this: when we set up this new government, who is going to be boss? The convention's answer was — nobody. This may seem like a decision to have no government at all, but that is not true.

Men who had been carefully studying all kinds of government — such men as Washington, Benjamin Franklin, Gouverneur Morris, Rufus King, John Dickinson, and, especially, James Madison and Alexander Hamilton — now came forward with what they had learned.

They were well aware that Englishmen had been fighting over the powers of government for more than six hundred years. The king claimed them. Parliament claimed them. Sometimes one grasped them, sometimes the other. On one occasion King Charles I marched into Parliament with a file of soldiers behind him and chased the members out at the point of a sword. Later Parliament raised an army of its own, defeated the king, and cut off his head. But the commander of Parliament's army, Oliver Cromwell, was as hard to handle as King Charles; when Parliament wouldn't do as he said, Cromwell, too, marched in with soldiers and chased the members out. So it had gone for years, Parliament sometimes holding all the powers of government, at other times the king holding them, but nobody had ever thought of splitting them up.

The men who made our Constitution pointed out that you should always say "powers" of government, for they are three — the power to make laws, the power to enforce laws, and the power to decide who is right when there is a dispute over what the law is. The law-making power is called the legislative, the law-enforcing power the executive, and the law-deciding power the judiciary. Put all three into the hands of one man and he will be an absolute king, boss of everything. Split them up and put each in the hands of a different authority and nobody will be boss; yet when the three authorities get together, all the powers of government can be put into use.

So the Constitution splits them up, giving the legislative power to Congress, the executive power to the President, and the judicial power to the Supreme Court. Each has authority in its own field, but each must attend to its own business and let the others alone. Congress cannot try lawsuits. The Supreme Court cannot appoint Cabinet officers. The President can neither make laws nor try cases.

The makers of the Constitution were determined

to fix things so that there would be no quarreling about who was to make law, who to enforce it, and who to decide disputes under it. So they set up a different authority to do each of these things and made them exactly equal in power, and any two could hold down the third if it tried to seize more than its share.

In our time this seems the natural thing to do and nothing to get excited about. But we must remember that it never had been done before in this way. It came to be called our system of checks and balances, meaning that two branches of government can check the third, and that the powers of the three branches are equally balanced against each other.

Nothing in the world is perfect, certainly not this system. Sometimes the balance has been upset. Sometimes the checks have failed to hold. But most of the time it has worked so well that under it the United States has become great and powerful, and in about one hundred and seventy-five years we have had only one big fight over the powers of government.

Then came the question of how to set up these three branches. About two of them there was no argument. Everybody agreed that Congress ought to consist of a large number of members elected by the various states, and that the Supreme Court ought to consist of a smaller number of judges, but more than one. However, when it came to the third branch, the executive, there was great argument. Some believed that to give one man power to enforce the laws would be just about the same as setting up a king, and they wanted a committee of at least three.

Others said that a man who could only enforce the law, but could not make it, could never be a king. They went on to say that the executive is different from both the legislative and the judiciary branches of government. In making a new law, one has to be very careful about the words used in writing it. So a lawmaker ought not to be rushed. He should have plenty of time to get the thing right. In the same way, when a judge is called on to decide a dispute under the law, he cannot hurry. He must listen to what both sides have to say. He must make up his mind which side is telling the truth, and if both are telling part of the truth, which is usually the case, he must decide which has the most truth on its side. This takes time; but it is far more important for a judge to decide justly than to decide quickly.

But the executive is different. The business of that branch is not to study, but to act. Suppose, for example, that a riot broke out in the city of Washington, and a mob attacked the ambassador of some friendly nation, as one did attack the Vice-President of the United States in South America in 1958. Suppose the police — they are part of the executive branch — instead of acting, spent time studying the various ways of acting in order to determine which was best. The man might be killed in the street before anything was done, and his nation might be angry enough to go to war about it.

Nothing like that is likely to happen, but some quick decisions have to be made every day. For instance, a member of the Cabinet may die or resign, leaving a great department without a head. The choice of a new one can be made more quickly by one man than if three have to get together and agree.

The convention of 1787 came around to the view that the executive branch of the government ought to have one head, so they wrote in the Constitution that the executive powers should be vested in, or given to, a president of the United States. They made it just one president, not three.

As for the number of judges in the Supreme Court, they left that for Congress to decide. The number has varied. We have had as few as five and as many as eleven; the number at present is nine.

The Constitution makers knew that it would be

impossible for one court to hear every little lawsuit in the country, so it declared that there should be lower courts to hear a case first, and the Supreme Court should hear only those in which one side claimed, and could show pretty good reason for claiming, either that the lower-court judge had made a mistake, or that the law itself was a mistake in that it was somehow against the Constitution.

There are two exceptions to this rule. If a state sues another state, no lower court hears the case. It goes straight to the Supreme Court. So does a case in which the ambassador of some foreign country is involved.

All this was fairly easily worked out, and so were many minor questions. For instance, it was agreed that we couldn't have thirteen different kinds of money in one country, so the United States alone was given the right to coin money that must be accepted in payment of a debt in any state. We couldn't have thirteen armies and thirteen navies, so the United States alone was given the right to maintain an army and a navy. We couldn't have business interrupted every time a man hauled a barrel of flour from one state to another, so that each state was forbidden to levy duties on goods from another state.

There remained the really tough problem — how

were the small states going to protect themselves against being robbed and oppressed, perhaps destroyed, by the large ones? The Articles of Confederation tried to solve this by giving each state one vote in Congress, but all that did was to leave the large states at the mercy of a combination of small ones.

Arguments about this went on all summer long and half a dozen times they almost broke up the convention. The debate centered around what was called the Virginia Plan, which called for a legislature of two branches, with members apportioned according to population, and the New Jersey Plan, which called for a single legislative body in which each state was equally represented. The Virginia Plan favored the large states, and the New Jersey Plan favored the small ones. The deadlock was broken by the Connecticut Compromise.

The compromise was very ingenious. It provided that Congress should consist of two chambers, and that no law should go into effect until passed by both and signed by the president; to one chamber, the House of Representatives, each state should send a number of delegates in proportion to the population of the state; in the other chamber, the Senate, each state should have two senators, each with one vote, and no state could be deprived of its two votes without its own consent. Together these two chambers make up Congress.

That was the really hard part of writing the Constitution of the United States. It looks so simple and plain to us today that we can't see why it took the wise men of 1787 all summer to figure it out. But nothing like it had ever been done in the world before and nobody could be sure that it would work.

A great many were sure that it wouldn't work, so many that for a time it was doubtful that the Congress — the old Congress existing under the Articles of Confederation, with its one-state-one-vote rule — would even submit the new Constitution to the states; and after it was submitted, it was doubtful that the states would ratify it. However, in September of 1787 the Constitution of the United States was presented to Congress, which sent it to the states to be accepted or rejected. In the course of time all accepted it, although Rhode Island, the last, did not ratify until May 29, 1790, nearly three years after the convention. It probably would never have been ratified without a gentleman's agreement that the first thing the new Congress would do would be to amend the Constitution. This amendment would not change anything in the original Constitution, but would add to it something usually called a Bill of Rights.

The first Bill of Rights was a series of promises made in England by William and Mary before they were allowed to take the English throne. It was a list of things that William and Mary pledged themselves not to do to any Englishman, great or small.

In 1760, William Pitt, a great orator, made a speech in Parliament and described one of these promises in language so dramatic that it has never been forgotten: "The poorest man may in his cottage bid defiance to all the force of the Crown. It may be frail, its roof may shake; the wind may blow through it; the storms may enter, the rain may enter, but the King of England cannot enter. All his forces dare not cross the threshold of the ruined tenement!"

It was agreed, then, that as soon as the Constitution had been ratified by nine states the new Congress would immediately submit to the states an amendment, or amendments, containing a Bill of Rights. The agreement was kept. The new Congress, as a matter of fact, submitted twelve amendments, ten of which were ratified.

The first eight of them are really the Bill of Rights, and each one states something that the government shall not do. Here are several of the most important ones:

The United States shall not tell any man how he shall or shall not worship God, or forbid him to say

what he thinks and have it printed, or to get together with others to criticize the government, provided this is done peaceably.

No policeman or other government officer can enter your house without your consent, unless he has a written order from a judge; and no judge shall issue such an order unless someone has sworn that he believes you are keeping in your house stolen goods, or someone who has committed a crime, or something else that is unlawful; and the judge's order shall describe the persons or things that the officer may seize; and he shall remove no others.

No person shall be brought to trial merely because somebody accuses him of a crime, but only after a grand jury has looked into the matter and decided that probably there is some truth in the accusation. Nobody once tried and found not guilty shall be tried again for the same offense. Nobody shall be beaten to obtain a confession of crime, or in any other way be made to testify against himself.

The government shall never take anybody's property for its own use without paying him what it is worth.

These things the government of the United States cannot lawfully do to any American, whether he is the richest man in the country or a homeless tramp.

So the powers of the government of the United

States have a limit, and that is a very important principle of the American system. Another important principle is that the sovereign power does not belong to any one man, but is divided among the people, and every man has a little of it. When more than half of the people get together, they possess most of the sovereign power; therefore, their will, as Thomas Jefferson said, "is in all cases to prevail."

This throws a great responsibility on the American citizen, and this responsibility makes him a little different from a man of any other country. Others can say, when things go wrong, "Well, the king's ministers did it, not I." They can say, as many Germans did say after the dreadful things done in the concentration camps were discovered, "Hitler did it. I had nothing to do with it." But not the American. The men who run the United States government were put there by his vote and are acting in his name; so whatever they do is done by his authority, and he is responsible for it.

Thinking about this is not pleasant. It is much nicer to be able to lay the blame on someone else when things go wrong, but an American can't do it. He must shoulder the blame himself; there is nobody to carry it for him. But suppose things go right, quite splendidly right. If you and I are partly responsible for what goes wrong, we are equally responsible for what goes right, and in this country of ours a great many things have gone right. When our government does the right thing, we have reason to be very proud.

CHAPTER THREE

Three Great Americans

AS SOON as the Constitution had been ratified by nine states, Congress ordered an election to choose a president, and members of the House of Representatives. The president was to choose the members of the Supreme Court, and the state legislatures were to choose members of the Senate.

Practically everybody in the country except George Washington agreed that Washington should be the president. He did not want this. He did not want anything except to settle down on his fine plantation at Mount Vernon and spend the rest of his days in peace and quiet. It is a beautiful place, on a high bluff above the Potomac River, at a point where it is two miles wide. Washington loved it, and he liked farming, especially such things as trying new crops or new varieties of old ones, seeing what would grow best in the Virginia climate, and what

could be done to make the soil produce more and
better grain and fruits and hay and tobacco. But
from 1775 to 1783, eight long years when he was
Commander in Chief of the American Army, he had
hardly seen the place except for a day or two at a
time.

His wife, Martha Washington, did all she could,
and he had overseers, of course, to keep the farm
going; but very few overseers take care of a farm
as well as the farmer himself does. When Washington got back to Mount Vernon at the end of the war,
he found weeds and bushes growing up in some of
the fields, gullies washing away others, some of the
fences broken down, barn roofs leaking, and things
generally in such a mess that it took him years to get
the place back in good shape again. Then, just about
the time when he got it back to what he thought it
ought to be, he was elected president and had to
leave again.

It was a great honor, but it didn't make him
happy. He would much rather have stayed at home
and let someone else have the honor. But it was
more than an honor. The country was starting on a
new kind of government that had never been tried
before, and unless it got the right kind of start it
could never succeed. Washington was the only man
in the country who could give it that start, because

he was the only one whom everybody trusted. Americans knew that Washington would not try to use the office of president for his own profit, and they were not so sure about any other man. So they needed him, and when his country needs him a great man never refuses to go.

The job proved worse than he had feared. Washington held it for eight years, from 1789 to 1797, and every day of those years he was worried about something. Much of the time he was angry because people were always doing stupid things or rascally things. Often he was disappointed when men whom he had thought able and patriotic turned out to be foolish and selfish. Very seldom did he enjoy being president. When he finally got out of the office, he told someone that he felt like a prisoner being let out of jail.

It was bound to happen that way, because a new country, trying a new form of government, cannot avoid a great deal of confusion and quarreling, and is lucky if it can avoid actual fighting. Washington had assistants, of course, and some fine ones; but just because they were first-rate men they had ideas of their own, and their ideas frequently clashed, which made more trouble for the President. Congress had divided the work of the government into four great departments, each headed by a secretary, whom the

President was to name. One department handled foreign affairs, and its head was called the Secretary of State; another handled money matters, headed by the Secretary of the Treasury; another, military affairs, headed by the Secretary of War; and the fourth, legal affairs, headed by the attorney general. There was also a postmaster general, but his was not a separate department until many years later; and the Secretary of War looked after the Navy as well as the Army. (Today there are ten of these departments, and the ten secretaries are called the President's Cabinet; six of the ten were added after Washington's time.)

When Washington became president on April 30, 1789, the United States was weak and it was poor. This made two questions very important indeed. One was, would the rest of the world let us alone? That was because we were weak. The other question was, if we were let alone, could we manage to keep going? That was because we were poor.

We had won the war against England, but everyone knew that it was because France had helped. England, France, and Spain were all very much stronger than we were, and if any two of them combined against us we would not have a chance. So it was important — very important — to keep them from combining. That was the business of the State Department.

We were poor because we had no way of using what we owned. We had an enormous quantity of land, but very few people to work it; and land that you cannot use does you no good. Coal is valuable, but not until you have dug it up. Iron and even gold and silver are of no value as long as they are buried in the ground. Our corn, wheat, tobacco, and other farm products, and our fish, furs, and timber were not wealth unless we could sell them, and to do that we had to have money and credit. This was the business of the Treasury Department.

So for Secretary of State and Secretary of the Treasury President Washington needed two of the best men he could get. He chose well. He made Thomas Jefferson, of Virginia, Secretary of State, and Alexander Hamilton, of New York, Secretary of the Treasury; and each did his work so well that they have been regarded ever since as among the very great Americans.

It would have been hard to find two men more completely different. Jefferson was tall, awkward, and ugly. Hamilton was small, graceful, and handsome. Jefferson's father was a civil engineer and farmer, not very rich, but prosperous. His mother was a Randolph, a Virginia family which, at that time, was rich and famous. Hamilton's people were poor. They lived on the island of Nevis, in the West Indies, and his father couldn't have been much good, because he left his family when the boy was very small. Jefferson's hair was almost red, his eyes blue, his face freckled. Hamilton was dark-haired, dark-eyed, dark-skinned. Jefferson's father was Welsh, Hamilton's Scottish. Jefferson hated making speeches from a public platform. Hamilton loved it.

But none of these differences mattered much. What really counted was the different way in which they looked upon the problem facing the new country — the problem of allowing the people to govern themselves without ruining the country. Hamilton saw it one way, Jefferson another, and each tried to persuade Washington to see it his way. All through the four years of his first term Washington tried to get them to agree, but he couldn't do it. At the end of the first year of the second term, Jefferson quit, and at the end of the second year Hamilton quit. But by that time the two of them, with Washington deciding now in favor of one, now of the other, had given the government the shape it still has.

The point at which they disagreed is not easy to explain. It is not hard to pick out one particular thing and find that Hamilton said we should do it one way, Jefferson the other. You can pick out a large number of such items; but when you have listed them all you still don't know *why* Hamilton said do it this way, and Jefferson said, no, do it the other way.

That *why* was a difference in the two men's way of judging people. Both Hamilton and Jefferson knew that some men are wiser and better than others. Both agreed that the wise and honest ones ought to run the country. But when it came to deciding where you are going to find the wise and honest ones, they split apart. Jefferson said that they are as likely to be found in one class of people as another. Hamilton said they are more likely to be found among the well-educated and successful than among other classes.

This may seem to be a small difference, but in fact it is a great one. It is a question that has never been answered once and for all. To this day there are Americans who believe that Hamilton was right, although the country has taken Jefferson's view, as far as the laws are concerned.

But it did not do so at first. Washington inclined, on the whole, to Hamilton's view. He knew, as everybody knows by the time he is grown, that the world is full of people who are honest in most things, and that there are a good many who are wise in most things, but the men who are both wise and honest in most things are scarce. The great problem of government, then, is to arrange things so that these people, although they are few in number, shall have most of the power.

Jefferson thought that the answer was to let all the people decide which among them are the wise and honest, because he believed that all the people could come nearer choosing rightly than any one man or any group of men could. Hamilton didn't believe it for a moment. He wished to arrange things so that the opinion of an educated man, or one who had proved that he was smart, would count for more than the opinion of an ignorant man who had never done anything that was a great success. He argued that the fact that a man has succeeded in business or in some profession proves he is intelligent; therefore he ought to have a greater say in government than others. Hamilton's way of putting it was that he wished to give most authority to "the rich and wellborn."

Jefferson's answer to that was that success in business proves that a man is smart, but doesn't prove that he is honest; and the fact that a man has been to college doesn't prove that he is wise. Therefore he was against giving any more power to the rich and wellborn than to others.

This difference was the beginning of all their disputes. When anything came up that seemed likely to give extra power to the rich and wellborn, Jefferson was against it. When anything came up that seemed likely to give more power to the ignorant and stupid, Hamilton was against it.

The people of the country were divided, some following Jefferson, others Hamilton, but in the beginning most followed Hamilton. In 1796 Washington refused to run for a third term, and the people elected John Adams of Massachusetts. He was a Hamilton man, or at least a member of the Hamilton group, who called themselves the Federalist party. Jefferson was elected vice-president. His followers first called themselves the Republican, later the Democratic-Republican, and many years later, the Democratic party.

While Washington was president, both Hamilton and Jefferson followed him and took their friends along; but after Adams was elected, the Federalists did not support him, but continued to follow Hamilton, while the Republicans followed Jefferson. This left the President a man without a party and he had an unhappy time. Hamilton and Jefferson were still opposed to each other and Adams could not make them agree. When he tried, Hamilton turned against him, and since Jefferson never had been for him, things got out of hand and nobody knew who was really running the government.

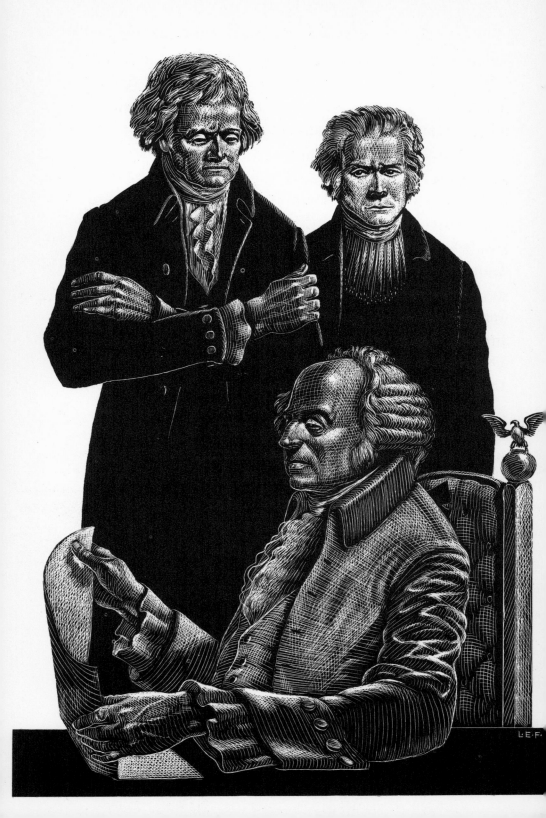

In France, revolution had broken out in 1789, and it did not stop, like ours, with overthrowing the king's government. It overthrew everything — the king, the nobility, the Church, and, to a large extent, even private property. The other kings of Europe united to put down the revolutionists, and that only made them worse; they cut off the French king's head, then the queen's, and then began cutting off the heads of everybody who stood up for the king and queen. The armies of the other kings marched into France but were whipped and thrown out, and it began to seem likely that the revolution would spread all over Europe.

What the French were doing caused as much excitement after 1789 as the Russian revolution did after 1917, and the French revolutionists were regarded in this country very much as the Communists were regarded after 1917. Some people hated them from the start, but some, noting such sensible things as their proclamation of equal rights, hoped that it would be a revolution like ours. One of these was Jefferson, who had been our minister at Paris when the revolution broke out.

But when not only the king and queen and most of the nobility were killed, but also thousands of people whose only crime was that they wanted to be reasonable, even Jefferson admitted that the thing had gone too far. However, he and his party saw no sense in sending an American army to try to stop it, and in this Adams agreed with them.

But Hamilton and his party did not. They did not believe that the American people were any more reasonable than the French people, and they were dreadfully afraid that if the thing was not stopped in France it would spread to this country, and we would soon be cutting off heads here as fast as they were in Paris. So they tried to push Adams into war with France.

This was a bad mistake, because John Adams was not the kind of man to be pushed around. He was little and fat and so vain that people often laughed at him, but he did what he thought was right and took no orders from anybody. Some French naval officers decided that there was going to be a war, and began to get very tough with American ships and sailors, and our people would not take it. There were at least four sea fights; in three we lost one ship and the French lost two, while the fourth was a drawn battle. But then the French government offered to settle things peaceably and Adams instantly agreed. The Federalists were so disappointed that they turned against Adams, and hated him as much as they did Jefferson.

Then the Federalists made another mistake. They passed a law making it a crime to criticize Congress or any government officer. This was flatly against the first article of the Bill of Rights, which says that Congress shall make no law of that kind. This was called the Sedition Law. At the same time, they passed a law giving the president power to put out of the country any alien whom he thought to be a dangerous man. This was the Alien Law. But the Constitution does not give the president or anyone else such power until the man has been proved to be dangerous.

Jefferson and his friends were strongly opposed to the Alien and Sedition Laws (which they later killed) and also to war with France. In 1800 the Democratic-Republicans voted for Jefferson for president, while the Federalists voted to re-elect Adams. Jefferson won, and the Federalists never elected another president.

That election showed one bad error in the Constitution. The rule was — and still is — that the people should not elect the president themselves, but should choose certain men, called electors, who should then elect the president. Each state should have as many electors as it has members of Congress in both House and Senate. It was provided that each elector should vote for two men and that the man with the largest number of votes should be president and the one with the next largest number, vice-president.

The second man on the Jeffersonian ticket was Aaron Burr, a New York lawyer and enemy of Hamilton; and when the electors' votes were counted Jefferson and Burr had exactly the same number, both receiving more votes than Adams.

In a case of that kind the Constitution says that the House of Representatives shall take one of the three highest men and elect him president; and the Senate, in the same way, shall elect the vice-president. Some Federalists saw a chance to beat their enemy, Jefferson, by electing Burr as president, although everybody knew that the people had really

voted for Jefferson. Hamilton hated Jefferson, but he despised Burr; so he urged his friends in Congress to vote for Jefferson. And enough of them did so that he was elected. That sort of thing cannot happen again, because the Constitution was amended to make each elector vote for one man for president and another for vice-president.

How right Hamilton was in disliking Burr became very clear later. In 1804 Aaron Burr, angry over an election in New York State, challenged Hamilton to a duel. Hamilton foolishly accepted, and was killed. Three years later Burr was brought to trial, not for killing Hamilton but for treason. He was accused of trying to split off the western part of the United

States and the evidence was strong, although not strong enough to prove that he had actually made war on the country, so he was acquitted. But even if he was not a traitor he was plainly a rascal, and it would have been shocking for such a man to be president of the United States.

This election of 1800 was very important because it set the pattern of politics that still exists — the people's habit of dividing into two main parties. There is no law about it. Anybody can set up a third party if he wants to, and it is constantly being done, but it is seldom that a third party gets enough votes to amount to anything.

The two big parties have not always stood for the same thing. In politics men do not always say exactly what they think, so sometimes you find a man, or a party, speaking one way and acting another. But in general there has been, ever since 1800, one party that worried more about the people's rights than about anything else, while the other worried more about law and order than it did about the people's rights. You can't really say that either was entirely right or entirely wrong. To have good government we must have freedom, and we also must have law and order. Which is the more important depends on what is going on at the time. If freedom is threatened, then to defend freedom is the important thing. If law and order are about to break down, then it is most important to look after them.

The great thing that was settled by the election of 1800 was the principle that whatever the majority voted for must be done. The larger part of the credit for this goes to Hamilton. He knew that the majority intended to elect Jefferson, and much as he disliked the idea he insisted that Jefferson must be made president.

Hamilton and Jefferson stood together on these two ideas: first, that the majority has a right to say what men shall and shall not *do;* second, that nobody not even the majority, has a right to say what men shall and shall not *think* and *say.* A man who does not believe these two things may be a citizen of the United States, born in this country and living here, but he is not a genuine American.

No two men in public life ever fought each other harder than Thomas Jefferson and Alexander Hamilton. Either would have been furious if anyone had suggested that they were working together. But they were. Together they were shaping the government into the form it has to this day; without either, the nation would probably have fallen apart long ago. If Hamilton had had his way, we might have drifted back into a kingdom. If Jefferson had had his way, our history might have been as stormy as that of the French since 1789. They checked and balanced each other and the result was a strong and steady government, yet the freest in the world.

They were enemies, but they respected each other. Hamilton insisted that Jefferson must be president; and many years later, when Jefferson placed in his house portrait busts of three great Americans, they were Washington, Franklin, and Hamilton.

CHAPTER FOUR

The Wheels Begin to Turn

WHILE Americans were busy shaping up a new kind of nation on this side of the world, in Europe, and especially in England, something was going on that turned out to be a great deal more important than the war against the king or any other war. Perhaps *something* is the wrong word. It was a great many things, thousands of things, each of which, taken by itself, didn't amount to much, but when they were added up they changed nearly everything in the world much more than war had changed anything.

This large number of little things all taken together made the great thing that we call the Industrial Revolution. It is not a very good name because *industrial* usually means having to do with the business of making goods, and this went much beyond that. Then *revolution* usually means rising up against the government and overthrowing it; but this affair wasn't aimed at any government. Yet although Industrial Revolution is a poor name, it is the best that anybody has been able to suggest.

It is impossible to say exactly when the Industrial Revolution began or exactly how long it lasted, but we usually say that it began about 1750 and lasted about a hundred years. There is a story that it began when a small boy in Scotland sat in the kitchen watching his grandmother's teakettle come to a boil. That is only partly true, because a great many other things helped it along; but it is quite true that the small boy did get an idea from watching the teakettle and, when he became a man, did do a great deal to change the world.

The boy's name was James Watt, and the idea was the use of steam to drive machines. James noticed that when the kettle of cold water was put on the fire the lid sat down flat; when the water started to boil, the lid began to bob up and down. Something was pushing it, and he wondered if there was any way to catch that force and use it.

A great many other people had wondered about the same thing. As far back as fifteen hundred years before James Watt was born, a Greek thinker named Hero, who lived in Alexandria, in Egypt, not only wondered about it, but showed that it could be done.

This Hero of Alexandria actually made a steam engine that would work — not very well, but after a fashion. Hero wasn't really interested, though. He made the thing as a sort of toy, and after he died it was forgotten.

James Watt *was* interested. As he grew up he kept thinking about it, and when he became a man he drew designs which he took to the best machine maker in England, William Boulton. Together they made a steam engine vastly better than Hero's, and much better than those of any others who had tried to make one.

You can't begin to understand how important this was until you stop to think how things had always been done before. The fastest way of traveling was by riding horseback. When Cornwallis surrendered at Yorktown, in Virginia, Washington wanted to get the news to Congress, in Philadelphia, as quickly as possible. So he sent one of his aides, Colonel Tench Tilghman, and Tilghman broke all records by getting to Philadelphia in seven days. Congress was so impressed that it gave him a fine horse and a handsome sword as a reward for his speed.

When George Washington wanted a sword, it was made exactly as swords had been made for Alexander the Great, who died two thousand years before Washington was born. Men beat the metal into shape with hammers, which meant that the greatest power applied at any one time was the power of a man's arm. When the wheat on Washington's farm was ready to be harvested it was cut by a worker with a small curved blade called a sickle, or a larger one called a scythe. It took much labor and much time to harvest a field that today's mowing machine could cut in a matter of minutes.

The sickle and scythe that Washington's field hands used were not much better than the tools used for harvesting wheat when the Bible story of Ruth, who gleaned in the field of Boaz, was written thousands of years ago. As long as it took a great deal of time and labor to raise even a little wheat, the farmer and his wife and children ate most of what was raised, and there was not much left to sell to people who lived in the towns; so a great many people had to work on the land or there would have been nothing for people who lived in the towns to buy. The towns and cities could not grow very large, because they had to get their food from the country nearby; and the country nearby could not produce enough food for many more people than the farmers themselves. When the first census was taken in 1790 the largest city in the United States was Philadelphia, and it had only 42,000 people. New Orleans existed, but it was not then in the United States, and it had less than 10,000 people. Chicago, Detroit, St. Louis, San Francisco, and Los Angeles either did not exist at all, or were merely small settlements in the wilderness.

Nevertheless, many people liked to live in towns, and in Europe they crowded into London and Paris in greater numbers than the surrounding country could feed, with the result that a large part of the city people were dreadfully poor and hungry most of the time. Thomas Jefferson saw this while he was in Europe as minister to France, and he came back feeling that large cities were as bad for a country as a cancer is for a man's body. He hoped that there would never be a large city in America and that most of our people would always be farmers.

The Industrial Revolution had already begun, but Jefferson had no idea what it was going to do in the next fifty years, for it moved slowly for a long time. First Watt and Boulton made steam engines that could drive heavy machines, such as flour mills, looms for weaving cloth, and trip hammers for forging iron. Men had long ago discovered that where there was a waterfall, or where you could build a dam and make a waterfall, you could build a water wheel under it and get power for mills and other machines. But you had to build your mill where there was a waterfall or a dam. A steam engine, though, could be set up anywhere, even in the midst of a city, where there were plenty of workers to tend the machines.

Up to that time thread to make cloth had been spun with a distaff held in the hand or attached to a spinning wheel. This was fairly light work, so it was usually done by women and young girls — mostly by the girls, since the housewife had too much else to do; and that is why to this day we call an unmarried woman a spinster. But in the same year, 1769, in which Watt got a patent for his steam engine, an Englishman named Arkwright invented a rack to which you could attach a dozen or a hundred distaffs and whirl them all at the same time, provided you had power enough to work it; and Watt's steam engine gave the power. Then a country preacher, the Rev. Dr. Cartwright, invented a loom that could be worked by mechanical power instead of by hand. One weaver could work one loom, but a steam engine could work a hundred, and all the weaver had to do was to supply the loom with thread and retie any thread that broke. One weaver could do this for many looms, so with the power machinery one weaver could make many times as much cloth as he could when he had to work the thing himself.

What happened in making cloth happened also

in making nearly everything else that people use. But Watt's engine stayed in one place and was good only for working machinery. Not until 1815 did a man named Stephenson build an engine that could move itself and pull a wagon after it. Large numbers of people went to work to make Stephenson's locomotive better and bigger, so that it could pull more and more wagons faster and faster.

The very first railroads were short bits of track built to haul heavy loads around factories, but they soon began to extend out into the country and to haul anything people wanted moved. It is interesting to note that the first regular freight hauled by the first American railroad of this kind was firewood,

brought to the city of Baltimore by the Baltimore and Ohio Railroad, in 1828.

This didn't happen all at once, and many years passed before most people realized that it was happening at all. They heard about the steam engine and then the spinning jenny and then the power loom and then the locomotive, and they were interested. But the ordinary American couldn't see how these things were going to make much difference to him.

In the first twenty-five years after the Constitution was adopted, most people paid less attention to these changes than they did to the doings of the great soldier, Napoleon Bonaparte. He started splen-

didly by saving France when all the kings in Europe had combined to wipe her out. But then, instead of imitating Washington and handing over power to the elected representatives of the people, he made himself emperor of the French and tried to become emperor of the world. He very nearly did it, too, but he was slowly worn down by the stubborn resistance of the British, who finally defeated him and kept him for the rest of his life on St. Helena, a remote little island in the South Atlantic.

During all the fighting in Europe in Napoleon's time, not many people were allowed to come to America. Yet the country continued to grow, because for every hundred people that died more than a hundred babies were born. At the start of the Napoleonic wars nearly all the people in this country had come — or their fathers, or grandfathers had come — from the British Isles. They spoke English and thought about things pretty much as the British did. After twenty-five years there were so many of them that, when the war ceased and people speaking German or French or Dutch began to come in, they had to learn English, instead of teaching the Americans their own language.

Napoleon was beaten in 1815, and within ten years after that the effects of the Industrial Revolution were being felt in a big way, although nobody understood them very well. The new factories needed workers living close enough to walk to them, and that meant towns. The towns needed food, and that meant roads to bring it in. But wagon roads were not enough to bring in food for a big town. So first they tried canals. A long one was dug from the Hudson River to Lake Erie, and immediately New York City began to grow tremendously, for in all the country around the Great Lakes you could put wheat or flour on barges and float it across the lakes, through the canal, and down the river to New York. So the city no longer depended for bread on the farms nearby.

Then came the railroads, and they made it possible to build cities far away from a river or a canal, for they could bring in everything needed from long distances, and very rapidly. Now for the first time it became possible to build and populate large cities without having most of the people hungry most of the time. Jefferson's idea that cities must be like cancers, because only the man who worked on the land could be really free and independent, was no longer true.

When a great war rages in the world it always happens that the neutrals are handled roughly by both sides. This was the case when Napoleon fought the allied powers. The United States, small, weak,

and far away from the center of the war, tried hard
to keep out of it, and for a long time managed to do
so. At first things went better for us than anyone
had expected. In 1803 there was a lull in the fighting and to prepare for the next war Napoleon
needed money. President Jefferson thought it a
good time to do a stroke of business, so he offered
to buy New Orleans, which Napoleon had taken
from Spain, for two million dollars. Jefferson was
amazed when the emperor said he would not sell
New Orleans alone, but he would sell all Louisiana
(which then included everything west of the Mississippi except Texas and California) for fifteen million dollars. Jefferson snapped up the offer. This

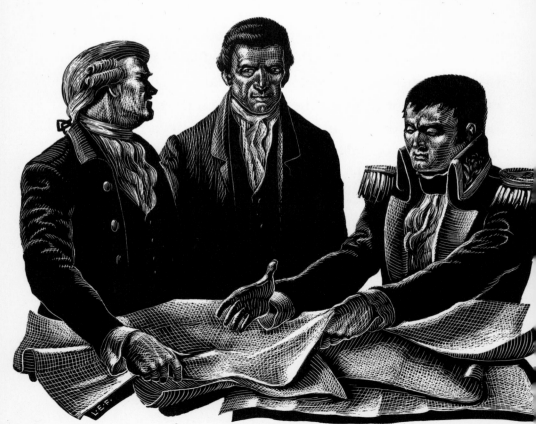

was the famous Louisiana Purchase, by which the United States gained land that later formed seven new states and parts of five others.

But things began to get worse and worse for the United States. First England and then France committed what seemed to us plain robbery and insult. Our ships and our citizens were treated very badly and the country grew more and more furious. Now by this time the men who had fought the Revolution were almost all gone. Washington, Franklin, and Hamilton were dead. Jefferson and John Adams were growing old and had gone back to live on their farms. Madison was president, and Congress was full of young men who had not themselves felt the power of the British Army. When these young men saw our ships seized and our seamen carried off to serve in the British Navy, they were too angry to think much about the odds. These War Hawks, as they were called, were determined to fight and, led by two brilliant young men — John C. Calhoun of South Carolina and Henry Clay of Kentucky — they pushed President Madison into war with Great Britain in 1812.

It turned out badly. We were not prepared for war, and we committed every kind of blunder. Fortunately for us, the British were so busy with Napoleon that they had to keep their best men in

Europe and the men they sent to America were second-raters who committed as many blunders as we did. Strange to say, we did best where the British were strongest; that is, at sea. We had only a few small warships and we could not fight the British main fleet in a great naval battle; but occasionally one of our ships would meet a British ship separated from the fleet, and in these small battles we did so well that after the war the British copied a good many of our ideas when they were building new frigates.

On land they tried the same three-pronged pincer movement that they had tried in the Revolution: one army coming down from Canada, another up

from New Orleans, while the third struck halfway between. But it failed again. The army from Canada was stopped at Plattsburg, in New York. The center force raided Washington and burned the Capitol and the president's residence, but when it struck at Baltimore it was beaten off. The southern army did not get started until the others were already stopped and then it was badly beaten by an American army under General Andrew Jackson in the battle of New Orleans.

As it turned out, that battle was really useless, because a peace treaty had already been signed at Ghent, in Belgium, two weeks before the armies met. But the news had not reached this country —

did not arrive until two weeks after the battle.

Some historians have said that this was a completely useless war, in which a great many men were killed for nothing. That is not quite true, however. The war did accomplish several things. It reminded each side that the other was a hard and dangerous fighter, much better to have on your side than against you. Then the long interruption of sea-borne traffic compelled the Americans to make for themselves a great many things they had been accustomed to bring in from Europe. In New England, especially, this was very important; it was at this time that factories began to be built all over New England, driven by steam power where there was no convenient waterfall. The Industrial Revolution was pushed forward rapidly, and by the end of the war New England depended more upon its factories than upon its farms, although it still depended more upon its ships than upon either factory or farm.

The War of 1812 is best remembered for two things that have nothing to do with fighting or business. One is the national anthem, "The Star-Spangled Banner." Francis Scott Key was inspired to write the song by the fight at Baltimore. The other is the name of the place where the president lives. It had been called simply "the president's residence," or sometimes "the presidential palace." When the British burned it, the limestone walls were not much damaged but were so blackened by smoke that they were hideous. When the interior was rebuilt the walls were painted white, and people began to refer to it as the White House. Many years later, when Theodore Roosevelt was president, he had his stationery printed with "The White House" at the top of the sheet. That made it official.

CHAPTER FIVE

Wild Man from Tennessee

WHEN Andrew Jackson won that great victory at New Orleans in 1815, of course he became a national hero and many people began to talk of him for president. When he ran the first time, in 1824, there were three other candidates in the race: John Quincy Adams, Secretary of State and a son of John Adams, Crawford of Georgia, and Clay of Kentucky. Jackson had more electoral votes than anyone else, but not a majority, so the House of Representatives had to elect a president from among the three with the most votes. That let out Clay, who ran fourth, and the House elected Adams, who immediately appointed Henry Clay as Secretary of State. Jackson's friends were furious. They said it was a dirty deal, a scheme to make Clay the next president, and they raised a tremendous uproar. In the next election, 1828, Jackson ran again and this time he defeated Adams by a large majority.

But there was much more to it than that. Jackson was a different kind of man from any of the presidents before him, and he was not chosen in the same way. Washington, Jefferson, Madison, and Monroe were all well-bred gentlemen from Virginia. Washington was very rich, and the others all had fine estates. John Adams and John Quincy Adams were lawyers from Massachusetts, not rich but well-educated men who had traveled widely and had been friendly with kings and noblemen in Europe.

Jackson was born of poor parents. His father died before his birth and his mother died while nursing American prisoners in a British prison ship during the Revolution. The boy first learned the trade of saddle maker, but later he studied law in the office of a judge in North Carolina and then set out for the new state of Tennessee. There he did extremely well; he made a fortune, became a judge, and then a senator, all the time acting as an officer in the state militia, which was taken over by the United States when the war of 1812 broke out. That is how Andrew Jackson happened to be in command at New Orleans.

But he never forgot where he came from and he felt his lack of education all his life. Even when he was President of the United States his spelling was terrible. Tennessee was the wild West in those days, and Andrew Jackson could be just as tough as any wild man in the state. He arrested more than one and he had a great many knife and pistol fights. He killed one man in a duel, and in another fight was himself wounded by a man who later became a senator from Missouri and one of Jackson's best friends. His name was Thomas Hart Benton. Jackson was certainly not like the learned, polite, and well-bred gentlemen who had been chosen as presidents before him.

The fact is that up to this time the common man had never done much in politics. He had left all that to the gentry. But in the new country of Tennessee there were no gentry. The people were pioneers, rough, bold, and independent, and they took no orders from anybody except a man who was rougher, bolder, and more independent than they were. When they did find such a man they admired him immensely and would do anything for him.

It had always been the custom for gentlemen in Congress to get together and decide who should run. The Jeffersonian Republicans would hold a meeting, called a caucus, and choose a man for their party; then the Hamiltonian Federalists would meet and choose a man for their party; and the common people went out and voted for one man or the other.

But there was no law about it; it was just a custom.
So the Tennessee legislature went ahead and nominated Jackson without waiting for any caucus, and
the common people elected him.

From that time on no man chosen by a caucus
was elected president, and soon the members of
Congress quit trying. In 1832, when Jackson decided to run for a second term, a big meeting was
held in Baltimore which was attended by all kinds
of people, not merely members of Congress, and this
meeting nominated him. They called it the national
convention of the party and presidents have been
nominated by national conventions ever since.

The caucus was not the only thing that Jackson
broke up. Another was the Bank of the United
States. This was the great bank in Philadelphia,
with branches in various other cities, where the government kept its money. As taxes and customs duties
and other charges due to the government were paid,
the money was deposited in this bank, and when the
government didn't need the money at once, the
bank could lend it to other people and charge them
interest. It was a neat arrangement and worked very
well, but it had one flaw — the government didn't
own the bank, yet the government money and government business made it by far the richest and
most powerful bank in the country. The govern-

81

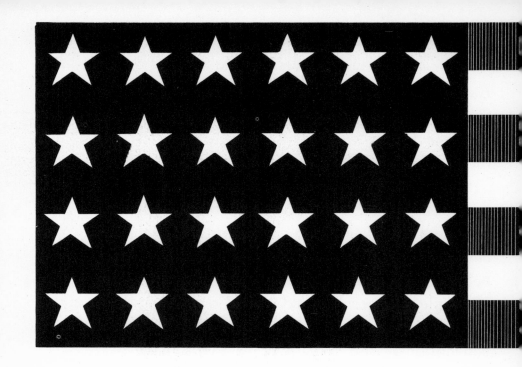

ment owned two fifths of the stock, but three fifths belonged to private persons, and in directors' meetings the three fifths could always outvote the two fifths.

Jackson thought that was bad. He felt that the rich men who held the bank stock could use the bank to help their friends and hurt their enemies; and he soon found that they looked on him as an enemy. So he decided to quit doing business through the bank. But the bank had many friends in Congress, among them Henry Clay and Daniel Webster, and these men put up a tremendous fight. In the end Jackson won, and the government business was given to other banks. Jackson was right about the bank, but he made many people angrier than they had been since the days of Thomas Jefferson.

They were so angry that they failed to see the really great thing that he had done. This was to put the idea in people's minds that the president is, or ought to be, the leader of the people and not merely the agent to enforce the laws that Congress makes. It is true that he has to swear, before he takes office, that he will enforce the laws, but Jackson felt that he ought to do more, that he ought to do his best to prevent the passage of bad laws, to work for the repeal of bad ones that had already been passed, and to suggest to the people ideas about improving the government.

Jefferson had felt the same way, but the other presidents had been inclined to sit back and let Congress lead. Ever since Jackson there has always been a strong feeling that the president is in a special sense the people's man. A district elects a representative, and he is the district's man. A state elects a senator, and he is the state's man. But all the people of all the districts and states elect the president, so he is their man.

That much everybody admits, but this question remains. Since he is the people's man, is it his duty to lead the people or to obey the people? Americans are still arguing about that, some taking one side, some the other. But there is really no final answer. It all depends on the president. If he is a strong man, he will lead and nobody can stop him. If he is a weak man, he will let others break the way while he follows along. Nearly a hundred years after Jackson another very strong president, Woodrow Wilson, said that the office is as big as the man who holds it can make it.

These, then, are the two things that Jackson did toward making Americans what they are: he killed the caucus and gave the choice of the president to the people; he made them feel that the president is more their man than are the heads of the other two branches, the Speaker of the House and the Chief Justice.

Through all these years the country was changing. Back in 1787, when the Constitution was written, most of the people had been farmers, so anything that was good for the farmers was good for most Americans. But fifty years later people in New England were more interested in manufacturing than in farming. New York, Philadelphia, and Baltimore had become large cities, interested in buying and selling and in importing and exporting. Maryland and Virginia raised much tobacco, but the rest of the South depended mainly on cotton. That is to say, each section had a specialty, and what was good for one was not always good for the others. New England, for example, wanted to buy cotton in the South, spin and weave it, and sell it back to the South as cloth. But so did the cotton mills in England, and sometimes the English could sell the same kind of cloth at a lower price, because their factories were better and their workers were paid less than those of New England. The same thing was true of other factory-made goods. The American factory owners persuaded Congress to impose duties on such goods brought in from abroad, and every new Congress made these duties higher. The duties were called the protective tariff. The South, which sold much of its cotton abroad, grew more furious each time it had to pay a higher price for manufactured goods imported from abroad. To the South, this was plain robbery; but to the North it seemed reasonable and right, because it allowed our factories to get a start against the bigger and better-equipped factories of England.

Finally, in 1828, Congress passed a tariff bill so high that it came to be known as the Tariff of Abominations, and the state of South Carolina revolted. The South Carolinians passed an ordinance declaring that as far as their state was concerned the tariff law was null and void and they would not obey it.

Now here was something that the Constitution had not foreseen and provided for. Everyone agreed that each state had a right to regulate its own affairs, but was the tariff its own affair? Andrew Jackson said that the laws of the United States were the supreme law of the land, including South Carolina. He ordered the United States Army and Navy to get ready, and arranged with a friend who lived in Charleston, a man named Joel Poinsett, to notify him the moment anybody interfered with an officer of the United States. Then he issued a proclamation, famous as the Nullification Proclamation, warning the South Carolinians that if they made a wrong move the Army and Navy would come down on them and every man responsible would be hanged.

For a moment it looked like war, for Jackson meant every word he said. Then Henry Clay, the great man of Kentucky, rushed in with a compromise by which the Tariff of Abominations would be gradually reduced. Congress still insisted on its right to make laws for the whole country, but things were smoothed over for the time.

So many things more startling than this happened later that most people long ago forgot the part that Joel Poinsett played in this business; but his name is still remembered for a curious reason. He had been minister to Mexico and he brought back to this country a plant never grown here before. It is the poinsettia, used everywhere now as a Christmas decoration.

The nullification business showed that things were not going well with the country, but nobody was wise enough to know what to do about it. The discontented South was led by John C. Calhoun. The satisfied North was led by Daniel Webster. Henry Clay, representing the West, stood between.

These men disagreed on almost everything else, but none of them wanted to see Americans fighting

each other, and as long as they lived they managed to avoid war. As late as 1850, when a break seemed almost certain, they arranged a compromise at the last minute. But Calhoun died in 1850, Clay and Webster in 1852, and that left nobody in Congress great enough to restrain the angry men on both sides.

CHAPTER SIX

Thunder Clouds

THE COMPROMISE of 1850 was an effort to smooth over a bigger event than nullification, an event that proved that things couldn't go on much longer in the way they had been going. This was the war with Mexico that broke out in 1846.

More lies have been told about this war than about any other that the United States ever fought. It was not that men meant to be liars, but that they could see only one side of the question. Yet when any big question comes up, there are always two sides and often many more than two, so a man who can see only one may be honest about it and yet entirely wrong.

The story is not simple. Mexico, having won her independence from Spain, took over all the land that Spain had held. This included not only what is now Mexico, but also what is now Texas, Arizona, New

Mexico, and California, with some parts of other states. The Mexicans, however, had not moved into this area. They had a few scattered settlements in Texas and California, but by far the greater part of the land was empty.

The part of the United States next to Texas was rapidly filling up, and the Americans in Louisiana and other places looked at all the empty land across the border and saw no reason why they shouldn't move in and make some use of it. At first, this was all right with the Mexicans, for land with no people on it is not of much use to any nation. But the Mexicans had never managed to establish a strong and just government. They had adopted a constitution much like ours, but they didn't stick to it. One dictator after another seized power and did pretty much what he liked, regardless of the constitution.

Naturally, this didn't suit the Americans living in Texas and they made trouble. They refused to obey laws, especially land laws, made by a dictator without consulting the Texans or, for that matter, anybody else. By this time there were so many of them that the Mexican government began to fear that they would take over the country. The dictator at the moment happened to be an especially bad and stupid one named Santa Ana, and he decided to stop any more Americans from moving into Texas, and to drive out those that were already there. But the upshot was that the Texans defeated him. A man named Sam Houston organized them into an army that whipped Santa Ana and drove him out of Texas, which then set itself up as an independent republic.

This happened in 1836. The United States took no hand in it, and for the next ten years Texas remained independent. But everybody knew that situation couldn't last, and the question was, would Texas be taken in by the United States or reconquered by Mexico or join some other power, probably Great Britain? At length Congress decided, on February 28, 1846, to admit Texas to the Union.

Santa Ana was furious and he decided to make trouble. Maps and surveys of those days were full of errors, and there was a dispute about the southern boundary of Texas. Mexico said it was the Nueces River, while the Texans insisted it was the Rio Grande, a hundred and twenty miles farther south. The row kept on and on until Washington finally sent General Zachary Taylor with an army, to hold the area. Mexican soldiers at Matamoras fired on the Americans across the river, the American officer turned his artillery on Matamoras and blew it to pieces, and the war was on.

It didn't last long. Santa Ana had much the bigger army, but it was badly armed and even more badly disciplined. General Taylor defeated it in three battles and drove it far to the south. But still Santa Ana wouldn't quit. So General Winfield Scott loaded another army on ships, landed it at Vera Cruz, and drove straight at Mexico City, which he captured after what was probably the most brilliant military campaign ever fought by an American general.

People in this country who opposed the war made light of it. They said it amounted to nothing because the Mexicans couldn't, or wouldn't, fight. But they did fight and fight hard. Buena Vista and Cerro Gordo, in particular, were bitter battles, and the final assault on Mexico City was a bloody affair. The Americans won because of the better equipment of

their men and the superior skill of their officers, not because the ordinary Mexican soldiers were cowardly or unwilling to fight. The men in the American armies learned a great deal about war in those campaigns.

Now Taylor and Scott had with them a large number of young officers, lieutenants and captains, who learned so much that later they became famous generals. Among them were Ulysses S. Grant, Robert E. Lee, T. J. (Stonewall) Jackson, George H. Thomas, P. G. T. Beauregard, Braxton Bragg, George B. McClellan, James Longstreet, George G. Meade, and the two Johnstons, Albert Sidney and Joseph E. You could almost say that the Mexican

War served as a rehearsal for the great Civil War that was soon to come.

But what it did at the time was to drive the two sections of the country farther apart. The Compromise of 1850 didn't really settle anything, not even the tariff, which it had reduced but not abolished. New England still wanted the protective tariff. The South still hated it. The West still wanted it on some things and didn't want it on others. This was perfectly natural, for a tariff that is good for a section that depends on factories is bad for a section that depends on farms. New England was depending more and more on factories, the South on farms, while the West was developing both. But it took a pretty wise man to see that this deep disagreement about the tariff was natural. Most men on both sides believed — maybe because they wished to believe — that the disagreement was not natural but had been fixed up by wicked fellows on the other side. When people want something and don't get it, they nearly always decide that the people opposing them are robbers. So they begin to hate each other, and when they begin to hate they are no longer reasonable.

In this case the South really didn't have a chance. In the first place it was weaker — six and a half million white people against twenty-three million in the

North and West — but what was far worse, it was trying to defend something that couldn't be defended. That was slavery.

Americans today know so well that it is not right for one man to own another man, as he owns a horse or a dog, that they can hardly believe anybody ever thought it was right. But one hundred years ago a great many people did believe it. There always had been slaves, and they took it for granted that there always would be slaves, and they didn't see anything wrong in doing what people had always done.

Even those wise men who knew that slavery was wrong felt about it very much as wise men feel about war today. They know it is wrong, but what are you going to do about it? One nation by itself cannot prevent war; all must agree. In the same way, one man by himself could not put an end to slavery. Even such wise men as Washington and Jefferson had owned slaves, although they thought it was a bad system.

Slavery had been bad from the beginning, but it got much worse after the Industrial Revolution. The slaves in America were practically all Negroes whose fathers or grandfathers had been bought from their masters in Africa or captured by slave traders. In the early years some Indians had been taken in war and made slaves, but they couldn't stand hard work in the fields and most of them either died or ran away. The Negroes were stronger; hard work couldn't kill them, and if they ran away where would they go? So by 1860 the word *slave* meant Negro in the United States, although there were many white, yellow, and brown slaves in other parts of the world.

When factories began to be built in New England, nobody knew much about handling machines driven by steam engines, and everybody had to learn. White men soon found out that they could produce more goods with machines than with hand tools, so they were willing to learn and did learn, very rapidly. But what good would it do a Negro slave to learn to manage a power loom? Whatever he made belonged to his master anyhow, so whether it was much or little made no difference to him. So he didn't learn, or he learned very slowly.

It was different on the farm. When crops were good, everybody on the farm, masters and slaves alike, had plenty to eat; when crops were bad, everybody had to skimp along on very little. So when the slaves worked well on a farm they were better off; which was a good reason for working. The same thing was true in a factory, but the slaves couldn't see it as plainly; so they never worked as well in factories as on farms.

White men decided that the Negro simply couldn't

learn to operate machines; so the New Englanders got rid of their Negroes. Some they set free, but most they sold to people who could use them on farms, and the larger number of these were Southerners. By 1860 most American Negroes and nearly all the slaves were in the states south of the Mason and Dixon Line, the boundary between Pennsylvania and Maryland.

Away back in 1787 the wise men who wrote the Constitution had known that slavery was an evil. The trouble was that they didn't know how to get rid of it. They knew that if they wrote in the Constitution that all men, Negroes and Indians included, should be free, they would never get as many as

nine states to ratify. They were not even sure that all the New England states would ratify, to say nothing of the South.

But they agreed, Northerners and Southerners alike, that if they couldn't end it, they would at least do what they could to slow its growth. At that time shipowners, including some from New England, were making a great deal of money by buying slaves on the coast of Africa, bringing them across the Atlantic, and selling them at a handsome profit in this country. The writers of the Constitution couldn't even put an end to that all at once, but they did write in a clause saying that after the year 1808 it would be a crime to bring another slave into the United States.

At that time nobody, except a few foolish men to whom most people paid no attention, thought this was a scheme to make one section of the country rich by oppressing another. Yet by 1860 that is exactly what the Southerners did think, or at least what they said they thought. Irresponsible men went around making speeches declaring that the New Englanders, having made all the money they could by selling slaves to the South, now wanted to take them away so that they could more easily rob the South by means of the protective tariff.

Equally foolish men in the North made speeches

saying that slavery was a scheme by which a few rich, proud, and lazy Southerners, living off the labor of black men, were plotting to rule the country and force slavery to be accepted everywhere. They said these men plotted the Mexican War, not to free Texas but to extend slavery into the West.

Both were partly right, because on each side there were a few rascally fellows doing exactly what the orators said they were doing. But both were mostly wrong, because the great mass of the people, both North and South, had no wish to try to rob or oppress anybody. The South had the worst of the argument, because slavery was a bad thing and was getting worse as the factory system continued to grow.

Added to everything else, there grew up in the North a group of people who were honest enough, but who thought so constantly about the evil of slavery that they couldn't see anything else. These were the Abolitionists, who stirred up more hatred than anybody else. The most famous of them, William Lloyd Garrison, once took a copy of the Constitution and, because it did not forbid slavery, burned it in public on Boston Common, calling it "a covenant with death and an agreement with hell." Such things as that disgusted reasonable men in the North, and they also gave the foolish element in the

South, called the "fire-eaters," more to talk about.

When we read about it now, a hundred years after it began, it is easy to see many ways by which the Civil War might have been prevented. At least we think it might have been prevented. We say *if* one man had been a little less stubborn, *if* another man had been a little wiser, *if* a third had known what the facts really were, then there would have been no war. But all these if's are doubtful. Perhaps those men had no choice. Perhaps they couldn't do anything else but what they did, or be anything other than what they were.

When an American living today says of the Civil War, "What a pity!" he is talking sense; if he says, "What a wicked thing!" he is talking nonsense. For a man is not wicked when he does what he honestly thinks is right. He may be mistaken. He may be foolish. He may be downright crazy and dangerous to everybody around him, but he is not wicked.

Still, even if you admit that it wasn't a clear-cut fight of good people against bad people, but terribly mixed up, you may say, "But why couldn't they see it coming, and why didn't somebody try to stop it?" They did see it coming and they did try to stop it, but they couldn't. Thomas Jefferson saw it coming, and John Adams, and many others who died long before the war began. As it got closer, many men tried to stop it and failed. There were four, in particular, whom we ought to remember with all honor because they tried their best, and did prevent war for many years. They were Henry Clay of Kentucky, Daniel Webster of Massachusetts, Thomas Hart Benton of Missouri (he was the man who shot Andrew Jackson), and Stephen A. Douglas of Illinois. They did not form an agreement; on the contrary, they often fought each other. But all of them looked on war as a calamity to be prevented at all costs.

People sometimes think of them as rather useless fellows, because they failed in the end; but the war might easily have begun in 1820 and they staved it off for forty years. To keep the country at peace for forty years is certainly not useless. In this case it may have saved the Union, for during those forty years the North and the West were gaining strength much faster than the South; yet when the war did come the South was beaten only after four years of very hard fighting. If they had fought earlier, the South might have won.

The Civil War did away with human slavery, and that was such a good thing that afterward people decided that getting rid of slavery must have been the object of the war from the start.

That is not true. At the start, every important leader on the Northern side said that he did not intend to interfere with slavery, and there is no reason to think that they were lying. If there had not been a single slave in America, there might still have been a war. There certainly would have been a contest of some kind, because there was a big question that had to be settled.

That question was whether this was to be one big country or a gang of small ones, working together in some things, but each going its own way in others. The Constitution had not settled this question, because you could read it either way. Its very first line reads, "We, the people of the United States" — not "these United States" — which would seem to mean one country. But the last paragraph of the Constitution, as it stood when Washington was president, said that any power not mentioned in the Constitution as given to the Federal government was retained by the states, or the people, which would seem to mean that this was one country in some things and several countries in everything else.

But even that was not clear. The words said that powers not mentioned were retained by the states "or the people." What people? There were the people of the United States. There were also the people of Virginia and the people of Massachusetts and the people of each of the other states. If it came to that, there were also the people of Philadelphia and of New York City and of Boston and of Baltimore.

An argument about this went on for years and years. Some people sided with John Marshall, Chief Justice of the United States, who said that the country was one country and therefore had the right to do everything necessary for a country to do. The party of Jefferson and Jackson disagreed, and at every election these two parties did all they could to persuade the majority to vote for their candidates. The parties had different names at different times. When Alexander Hamilton was alive his party was called the Federalist party. Marshall, being a judge, never actually led the party, but he thought pretty much as Hamilton did, and in his time the party took the name of Whig; it later became the Republican party. Jefferson's followers called themselves first Republicans, then Democratic-Republicans, and then, after Andrew Jackson's time, plain Democrats, which they have remained to this day.

John Marshall, Thomas Jefferson, and Andrew Jackson were all great men, but not great enough to settle the argument. It was settled slowly and gradually by events over which they had no control.

For one thing, people were swarming into the country, making it more thickly settled. At the same time new machines were being invented and factories were building up the cities. Roads were being extended and made better and better. Then came the canals and then the railroads. Finally Congress gave a portrait painter by the name of Morse a grant of $30,000. He strung an iron wire from Washington to Baltimore, and with some electric batteries and magnets sent over it a message that could be understood at the other end. The first message, except, of course, for a lot of testing, sent over the electric telegraph was a line from the Bible, "What hath God wrought?" It was received at Baltimore in 1844.

Now think what this meant. The country was still huge and sprawling, but distance no longer meant

much when you could travel with the speed of a railroad train; and it meant still less when you could send a message from Charleston, South Carolina, to Boston, Massachusetts, with the speed of lightning. It was still thinly settled, if you compare it with England, but people were pouring across the Mississippi River and a few had crossed the Rocky Mountains into California.

Some people realized that when the country changes, ideas about the country must change too. But many Americans felt that whatever such men as Hamilton or Jefferson had said must be true not only when they said it, but for all time; so they refused to think for themselves.

That was the real reason for the great war that almost destroyed the country. Look at it one way, and you can say that it was nobody's fault. Look at it another way, and you can say that it was everybody's fault. It was the result of trying to run the country by a set of old rules that would no longer work. Yet they were good rules in the beginning and had worked well for more than half a century. The trouble was that they had been made for the kind of country this was in 1787, and by 1860 it had changed into a different kind of country.

So hatred kept increasing and good sense and truthfulness kept shrinking until 1860, when the South took the desperate — indeed, insane — course of trying to break away from the Union and set up a government of its own.

CHAPTER SEVEN

Storm over the Land

THE WAR that followed was the fiercest and bloodiest ever fought by the United States, and one of the fiercest and bloodiest of modern times. In it Americans were fighting Americans. It was a sort of family fight, and a family fight is usually the worst kind.

In the armies on both sides there were about two and a half million men, and half a million were killed in battle or died in camp. That meant one man out of every five was killed. In World War I, in which the United States fought during 1917 and 1918, we lost one man out of every twelve, and in the longer World War II, 1941-45, we lost one out of eleven.

The Civil War lasted four years, from 1861 to 1865. The reason for that was that although the South had fewer men and fewer guns, ammunition, and other supplies, it had some officers who were brilliant strategists. Robert E. Lee was the great general of the South, but he had under him others who were nearly as good, especially Longstreet, the Johnstons, the Hills, and above all, Stonewall Jackson. Jackson got his nickname in the first big battle of the war, Bull Run. In that battle part of the Confederate line began to give way, but the part under Jackson did not; so the general whose men were beginning to retreat called on them to rally, shouting, "Look at Jackson, standing like a stone wall!"

Again and again the Southern generals, by swift and skillful movement, were able to bring their whole force against part of the Northern army and cut it to pieces before the rest could get there. Twice Lee invaded the North, but both times the Northern commander managed to bring up his army and stop him. General McClellan did it at Antietam, in Maryland, and later General Meade did it at the great battle of Gettysburg, in Pennsylvania. But Lee, although stopped, was not beaten either time, and managed to get his army back into Virginia.

The North did not really begin to win until it gave the supreme command to a soldier who had been fighting in the West, that is, in Tennessee and Mississippi. His name was Ulysses S. Grant. At the battle of Shiloh, in Tennessee, Albert Sidney Johnston fell on part of Grant's army and wrecked it before Grant could come up with the rest. But at a critical moment in the battle Johnston was killed, and in the confusion that followed Grant had time to get there with the rest of the army and save the day.

Grant was the first Northern general to realize that the way to deal with the Southerners was simply to wear them down, no matter how many men it cost. When he was appointed to the supreme command, he turned the western army over to General William T. Sherman with orders to get in behind Lee through Atlanta, in Georgia, while Grant went at him from in front. Grant's plan was simple. It was just to keep on fighting, no matter how often he might be defeated or how many men he lost. He knew that he could always get more men and that Lee couldn't.

The last campaign was the most terrible in American military history. It started near Chancellorsville, Virginia, and moved down the Rappahannock River, with Grant trying to cross and Lee throwing him back in battle after battle, with frightful losses. All the summer of 1864 it went on, like a gigantic dance, the two armies swinging together and swinging apart, swinging together and swinging apart, and all the time shuffling sidewise down the river. But every time they swung together a great many men

died, more of Grant's, but some of Lee's; and every time they moved down the river, they were getting closer to Richmond, the Southern capital.

At Cold Harbor Grant lost twelve thousand men in thirty minutes; but that did not prevent him from attacking again ten days later and losing eight thousand more. This strange dance of death ended at Petersburg, the fortress protecting Richmond, where Grant, after trying for four days to take the place by assault, settled down to a siege that lasted nine months. Grant had lost more men that summer than Lee had in his whole army, but fresh troops kept coming to Grant and almost none to Lee; so at Petersburg Grant had more of an army than he started with, while Lee had less than half of his left. Early in April Lee gave up Petersburg and Richmond and tried to move west, but General Sheridan blocked him. Then he tried to move south, but Sheridan blocked him again. The end came at Appomattox Courthouse where Lee, with Union armies on all sides, surrendered on April 9, 1865.

In the meantime General Sherman had not only cut through to Atlanta, but had marched right across Georgia to Savannah, on the Atlantic. This was the famous march to the sea that inspired the soldiers' song, "Marching through Georgia." Then Sherman turned north to join Grant, driving General

Joseph E. Johnston before him. Near Durham, North Carolina, Johnston surrendered and the Civil War was over.

Again in this war, as in the Revolution, it wasn't the fighting that made us Americans, except in the political sense. The fighting did decide that this is one nation, that no state or group of states can split apart. After that war no one doubted that a law enacted by Congress, provided it does not violate the Constitution, is law in South Carolina, in Massachusetts, and in every other state, no matter what the state legislature may do. That is to say, the Civil War killed secession and nullification, and they have never come to life again.

The fighting also put an end to slavery, but it did not make the former slaves first-class citizens. Congress tried to do that by law, but the people wouldn't back it up and for nearly a hundred years there have been laws in some states that restrict Negroes in certain ways, and in all the states there are customs that work against the Negroes, even when the law does not.

But this war, again like the Revolution, did one thing that was more important than any change in the laws. It gave Americans a second hero who, like George Washington, was a picture of what an

American ought to be and can be. The name of this one was Abraham Lincoln.

He was born in Kentucky, but when he was still a child the family moved to Indiana and, when the boy was fourteen, to Illinois. They were very poor, too poor to send him to school except for a short time. As soon as he was big enough he had to help with the farm work, and he did more and more of it as he grew larger and stronger. He was healthy and the hard work developed his muscles. He was six feet and three inches tall and always rather skinny, but he was very strong, much stronger than he looked. When he was a young man he was well known for the speed with which he could split logs to make fence rails, which was about the hardest work done on a farm in those days.

His mother died when he was twelve and his father married again. His stepmother was kind to Abraham and helped him all she could, especially with his books. When his school days were over he read every book he could get, and in that way he learned more than many boys do who go to school every day. When Lincoln became a young man he went to town, worked at whatever he could find to do (he once went with a flatboat down the Ohio River to the Mississippi and down that to New Orleans), but always kept on studying. At last in

Springfield he found law books and learned enough to become a lawyer. At this he was very good indeed, and soon became one of the best lawyers in Illinois. He married Mary Todd, a girl of a good family from Kentucky, and he might easily have become a rich man by doing nothing but practicing law.

But he didn't want to be merely a lawyer, even a rich one. He wanted to take part in running the country. When he looked around him he saw a great many things that he thought were wrong, and he wanted to do something about them. He was elected to the state legislature and afterward to Congress for one term; then he went back to the law.

One thing Lincoln didn't like was slavery. He did not feel that anyone had a right to go into the South and take the slaves from their masters; but he did not want slavery to spread into Illinois or into the new states in the West, and he came to believe that that was what the South was aiming at.

In 1858 he made his views known. Stephen A. Douglas was then a senator from Illinois, but his term ran out in 1858 and he hoped to be re-elected. Douglas was a Democrat, a party stronger in the South than it was in Illinois, and Douglas naturally didn't want to say anything that would hurt his party in the South. So Lincoln decided to run against him. There was no radio in those days, and candidates went about from town to town making speeches in which they tried to persuade people to vote for them. Lincoln and Douglas agreed to speak from the same platform on the same day in a number of Illinois towns, and every time they met Lincoln demanded that Douglas say whether he was in favor of stopping slavery from spreading over the whole country. Douglas finally had to say that he was in favor of stopping it.

Douglas was re-elected senator, but these debates did two things. In the first place, when Douglas had to say that he favored stopping the spread of slavery, he made the South — or at least its political leaders — furious. In the second place, the debates showed that Lincoln was such a splendid speaker that people all over the country wanted to hear him and began to think about what he said.

The Republican party at that time was a new one. It had been organized in 1856 and was composed in part of Democrats who didn't like slavery, and Whigs who didn't like either slavery or Democrats. In 1860 this new party nominated Lincoln for president. The Democrats nominated Douglas, but this made the Southerners so angry that they went off and nominated a man of their own, named Breckenridge. Finally some of the old Whigs and some Southerners who were more worried about breaking

up the Union than they were about slavery, nominated a man named Bell.

In the election Lincoln got more votes than any of the other three, although taken together they had a million more than Lincoln. This gave the South a chance to argue that Lincoln had not been honestly elected, since he did not get a majority of all votes cast. So, with this pretext, eleven states led by South Carolina, split off and formed what they called the Confederate States of America, with its capital first at Montgomery, Alabama, and later at Richmond, Virginia, and with a man named Jefferson Davis as president. Davis had been born in Kentucky, not many miles from Lincoln's birthplace, but he had lived for a long time in Mississippi, as Lincoln had in Illinois. The states that followed South Carolina out of the Union were Virginia, North Carolina, Georgia, Florida, Alabama, Mississippi, Louisiana, Tennessee, Texas, and Arkansas.

The president before Lincoln was a nervous old fellow from Pennsylvania named James Buchanan. If he had acted as swiftly and sternly as Andrew Jackson had done, he might have stopped the whole secession movement before Lincoln got to Washington. But James Buchanan was neither swift nor stern. He couldn't make up his own mind. He talked of this and he talked of that and ended by doing nothing important. He fluttered about until everybody, North and South, was disgusted and decided nothing could be done until the new man came in.

So when Lincoln was inaugurated, March 4, 1861, he found a nation already divided and on the brink of war. This was the last thing he had expected or desired; in fact, it was the very thing he had entered politics to try to prevent. To be sure, he was against slavery, but first and foremost he was against breaking up the Union. A year later, with war already raging, he wrote to the famous editor, Horace Greeley, that if he could save the Union without freeing a single slave, he would do it; or if he could save it by freeing all the slaves, he would do it; or if he could save it by freeing some and leaving others alone, he would do that.

That was the way most of the people in the North and the West felt in 1861. They were against slavery and they weren't going to have it in their own states, but as for fighting a war to free the slaves in other states, that was a very different thing and not many favored it. What they did favor was holding the Union together; but there were many different ideas about how best to do that. When Lincoln got to Washington everybody was talking at once and all of them were saying different things. The confusion was complete.

What pulled them together was the impatience of the Confederate general, Beauregard, at Charleston, South Carolina. In Charleston harbor there was a fort called Sumter, held by Major Anderson and a few men of the United States Army. Beauregard called on Anderson to hand over the fort to the state of South Carolina, but Anderson wouldn't do it without orders from Washington. They dickered and argued for weeks and months, but Anderson would not budge; and finally Beauregard grew so angry that on April 12, 1861, he ordered his artillery to blast down the walls of the fort and so compelled Anderson to surrender.

As it happened nobody was killed in this affair, but that wasn't the point. At Fort Sumter the Confederates had fired on the flag, and that was something about which the North would fight. The feeling was not all in the North. Four of the slave states — Delaware, Maryland, Kentucky, and Missouri — would not stand for firing on the flag, and they stuck to the Union. Even Virginia, North Carolina, Tennessee, and Arkansas hesitated, and North Carolina did not secede until May 20, more than a month after Fort Sumter fell.

So the North was united on the war, but it was far from united behind Lincoln. As we look back on it today it is hard for us to understand how people could have misjudged that man so badly. They knew he was a smart lawyer and an even smarter politician, but almost nobody believed that he had the kind of sense, and especially the kind of character, that a man must have if he is to handle really great issues. They thought he was a tricky fellow who had become president more by accident than by the power of his brain.

Lincoln had appointed to his Cabinet some very able men, which was fortunate; but practically every one of them thought that he knew more about running the country, and especially about running a war, than Lincoln could possibly know, and that was unfortunate. As for Congress, it did not merely *think* that it knew better than the President what ought to be done, it was dead certain. The result was that Lincoln had a terrible time getting his orders obeyed; and that is one reason why it took so long to win the war.

But little by little, as time passed, the people began to see what a wonderful man he was. He was patient — some thought too patient — with quarreling generals and Cabinet members. He hated war, but once in it he drove straight ahead and never for one moment thought of anything but winning. He did whatever he thought was necessary, although he often disliked what he had to do. He did not think

that the Constitution gave him any right to interfere with slavery in the South, but at last he decided that the North would fight harder, and he hoped the South would be hampered, if he did. So when the North at last won a real victory in the battle of Antietam, he issued a proclamation which said that the slaves in any state which did not lay down its arms and come back into the Union by the first of January, 1863, would be free. This was the famous Emancipation Proclamation. It did spur the North to greater effort, though it had no effect on the South, and the war went on for another two years.

The greatest thing that Abraham Lincoln did was to keep his head, and never let anger and hatred run away with him. When everybody else forgot, he remembered that most of the men in the Southern armies honestly believed that they were fighting for their own freedom, not to keep the Negroes in slavery. Less than a third of the white men in the South owned any slaves and less than a fifth owned more than two or three. The common soldiers of the South really believed that they were fighting to protect their homes, and Lincoln respected that; he knew that they were mistaken, but he did not think that they were wicked, and he hated the very thought of revenge.

Throughout the war he did everything he could

to keep down bitterness, and as a result a great many people in the North thought he was "soft" toward the South. Others thought he was too stubborn. In the election of 1864 he got only fifty-five out of each one hundred votes in the North; the other forty-five went to General McClellan, who was running against him.

Through it all he never changed. He was blamed for everything, including the good things he did and the bad things other people did, sometimes directly against his orders; yet he very seldom blamed anyone else. When men railed at him furiously, he turned their words aside with a joke; and that usually made them angrier than ever. Some people he thought were his best friends turned against him and worked behind his back to defeat him. He said no bitter word about them. "With malice toward none, with charity for all" was his motto, and he lived up to it.

When he spoke in public it was never to stir up fury; it was always to remind people of what America ought to be and could be. Three times — in his two inaugural speeches and in the great Gettysburg Address — he did this so wonderfully well that it has never been done better. The Gettysburg Address, delivered on the day when that battlefield was dedicated as a national memorial, lasted only about five minutes, but many critics agree that it is the greatest political speech ever made in America. It is now carved on the walls of the Lincoln Memorial in Washington.

Five days after Lee surrendered, an actor named John Wilkes Booth crept up behind Lincoln as he was watching a play in a Washington theater and shot him in the head. He died early the next morning, April 15, 1865.

His death undid, in an instant, a great deal of his good work. The grief and wrath of the North were so terrible that for a time they swept everything else out of men's minds. Booth escaped from the theater, but was pursued and shot to death — some think he

shot himself — in a barn in Virginia. Eleven of his friends were rounded up and four of them, three men and a woman, were hanged, although there is grave doubt that the woman knew anything about the plot.

Booth was probably crazy, and he certainly had no connection with any of the Southern leaders, who were horrified when they heard of his crime. But the South was blamed and, after all, what could you expect? A great and good man had been foully murdered, and when that happens it is hard for the best of men to remember that he should act "with malice toward none, with charity for all."

Lincoln's murder opened the way for those men in Congress who had always been opposed to his mild policy. Some of them were honest but bitter-minded men who thought more of revenge than they did of the country's good. Others were simply politicians who thought they could remain in power as long as they could keep the South out of the Union. Together they were a majority in Congress and when the new President, Andrew Johnson — he had been Vice-President at the time of Lincoln's death — tried to carry out Lincoln's policy, they impeached him and came within one vote of removing him from office.

These men pursued a harsh policy toward the

South. They called it reconstruction; actually it was destruction. Jefferson Davis was arrested and kept in prison for two years, part of the time in chains, without trial. The North had fought four years to prove that the South could not leave the Union; Congress now decided that it *had* left and was conquered territory. So the eleven states were for a time abolished and divided into five military districts, ruled by an army of occupation. It was ten years before the last of this army was withdrawn.

For several years after 1865 the South had a really rough time. The army of occupation was not nearly as bad as another sort of army that came behind it. These were the carpetbaggers — so called because the Southerners said they brought everything they had in the world with them in a carpetbag, a kind of traveling bag fashionable at the time. The soldiers were supposed to stay and keep order until new state governments could be organized and readmitted to the Union. The soldiers did their part pretty well; it was the carpetbaggers who caused the trouble.

A few of them were simply businessmen who wanted to get things going again, and they were all right. Most of them, however, fell into two classes. One was made up of honest fanatics who thought of themselves as missionaries whose duty it was to help the former slaves take over the South, in spite of

129

the fact that very few of them could read or write, and none of them knew anything about business and government. The other class was made up of rascals who didn't care a hoot for the slaves or anything else except the money they could make. These combined with the same sort of rascals born in the South — called scalawags — and together they persuaded the Negroes and the more ignorant whites to vote them into office. Once in, they proceeded to steal everything they could lay hands on. They did more lasting damage than Sherman had done on his march to the sea, although it was his aim to devastate the country in order to prevent the Confederate army from getting food.

And yet as we look back on it today we can see that reconstruction, bad as it was, was a great deal better than what has happened to other countries defeated in a great war. The only war criminals hanged were a few men in charge of notoriously bad prison camps. No civilian hostages were stood up against a wall and shot. There were no massacres. There were very few atrocities committed by drunken soldiers, and when a murder was committed the murderer was usually hanged by his own commander. The fact is, the South got off lightly by comparison with, say, Poland or the part of Russia overrun by the Germans.

After all, Lincoln's work was not entirely in vain. In spite of the wounds it had suffered and in spite of the crime of Booth, the victorious North did not altogether forget his reasonable and merciful spirit; and that is why the Union was restored as soon as it was, and so firmly cemented this time that it can never be broken again.

CHAPTER EIGHT

Money Grabbers and Money Givers

ONCE the fighting ended, most people, in the North and in the South, felt that the best thing to do was to forget it and go to work rebuilding the country. Perhaps the fierceness of the war had something to do with this. In 1861 the North did not really believe that the South would fight, and the South did not believe that the North could fight. Both were wrong. By 1865 the men in the gray uniforms of the Confederacy and in the blue uniforms of the Union had to admit that their opponents were brave men who fought well; and they had a high respect for each other.

Most of the bitterness was in the minds of those who stayed at home and never saw a battle; but even that subsided as time passed. Only two years after the war a Northern poet, Francis Miles Finch, read that the women of Columbus, Mississippi, had gone out to the military cemetery near that town on Memorial Day and had placed flowers on all the graves, Union and Confederate alike; and he wrote a poem that became famous because it expressed the feeling of a large part of the country. The last stanza read:

No more shall the war cry sever,
   Or the winding rivers be red:
They banish our anger forever
   When they laurel the graves of our dead!
Under the sod and the dew,
   Waiting the Judgment Day,
Love and tears for the Blue,
   Tears and love for the Gray.

Robert E. Lee became a hero in the North, and Abraham Lincoln became almost a saint in the South. And why not? Both were great men who sacrificed all that they had for their country; and both were Americans.

It was a fine thing that we could and did forget so desperate a quarrel so quickly; but it was not so fine that we forgot a great many other things besides the quarrel.

One thing that we forgot was the ideal of America

that Washington and Lincoln had set up for us. People sometimes say that Washington made us *a* nation among the other nations, and that Lincoln made us *one* nation among ourselves, which is true, in a way. They both also taught us that no nation becomes great until most of its people are willing to give to it more than they get from it — even their lives, if necessary.

This is what we are always forgetting and always getting into trouble by forgetting. We forgot it almost completely in the twenty years following the Civil War. (Some people still insist on calling it the War between the States, but the North won, and that made it a Civil War, which is a war inside one nation; if the South had won, it would have been a war between separate states, but the South didn't win.)

Another thing Americans came near forgetting after Lincoln's death is that when elections are held you must really try to find out who is the best man, and vote for him. The result was a great downswing in government, which was a shameful thing. It reached the lowest point after 1868, when the people elected U. S. Grant president, not because he knew anything about running the country, for he didn't, but because he was a great national hero. He was a fine soldier who had beaten the effort to break up the Union, and he deserved to be admired and thanked and rewarded. But electing him president was a poor way to reward him because, while it is a great honor, it is also a very hard job calling for training and skill that Grant didn't have.

He was an honest man, and he made the mistake of thinking that all the party leaders were as honest as he was. Some were, but some were not. Grant made a former brigadier general, named Belknap, Secretary of War, and later it was discovered that Belknap was taking bribes to keep certain rascals in office. Grant's private secretary, Babcock, was associated with men who were stealing from the government by selling whisky without paying the taxes on it. Grant himself appeared in public in company with a notorious stock gambler named Fisk, and some of his own family tried to get him mixed up in one of Fisk's dishonest deals — and almost did.

So for the first time in American history crooks could be found plotting crooked deals in the White House itself, because the President didn't know enough about politics to recognize a scoundrel when he saw one. It wasn't all Grant's fault. The people themselves were largely to blame for putting him in a position that he was not trained to fill.

Things were never quite as bad as that after Grant, and at least one president, Grover Cleveland,

135

insisted on common honesty in government. But no president for many years did much to explain to the people what new laws and new methods were needed by a new kind of country. One reason, no doubt, is that most of them didn't realize that it was a new kind of country, which is to say that they were men who lacked what we call vision.

During the war the North had had to build a great many factories to supply the army with cannon, rifles, bayonets, ammunition, uniforms, blankets, tents, wagons, and a thousand other things that an army must have. It had also built railroads at a furious rate in order to move the troops quickly to the places where they were needed; and it had built cars and locomotives in great numbers. In the West many thousands of acres of what had been empty prairie had been turned into farms to supply food for the soldiers, and hay and grain for the army's horses and mules — there were no gasoline-driven trucks in those days — as well as the horses and mules themselves.

So when the war ended, the country, and especially the North and West, had great quantities of tools and machinery and a million strong men, the former soldiers, to work them. In addition to that, it had a million or so square miles — not acres, miles — of empty land, much of it fine farm land and some

of it having under the surface immense quantities of
coal, iron, tin, lead, gold, silver, and other metals, as
well as oil. Of course at that time oil was not much
used except as kerosene in lamps.

Here were men, here were tools, here was land —
the three things necessary to create wealth. So the
country started in to create wealth, and did it at a
rate that nobody would have believed possible before the war. By 1869 one could travel from the
Atlantic to the Pacific by railroad, and after that
the West developed at a tremendous rate.

This was splendid, but in a little while things began to show up that were a long way from splendid.
A great many men were making a great deal of
money very rapidly, and soon some got the idea that
there was nothing in the world worthwhile except
making money; and from that it was a short step
to thinking that it was a good thing to make money
no matter how you made it.

It was that kind of thinking that made this period
a shameful one in American history in spite of all the
fine things that were done to build up the country.
Some shrewd fellows found that they could get
money faster by stealing it than by producing goods,
and they stole at a scandalous rate. Many others
found that without actually stealing they could make
fortunes by business practices that were unfair, yet

not forbidden by law; so they proceeded to act unfairly.

The trouble was that things were changing so fast that the law could not keep up with them. Perhaps it is better to say that it was not the law, but people's way of thinking that fell behind; for the law sets down in writing what honest men think ought to be done. When a man — more often a number of men formed into a company — built a railroad, most people thought it all right for him to charge whatever he could get for hauling freight and passengers. It was his railroad, wasn't it? It took a long time for us to realize that soon after you build a railroad a great many people along the line come to depend on

it to get their goods to market; so if you charge them an outrageously high rate you are really taking away from them part of what ought to be theirs.

Worse than that, if you charge one man a low rate and all his rivals a high rate, you are helping the first man put all the others out of business, because he can sell his goods for less than they can and still make a profit. Yet a man who owned a big factory that shipped a great deal of freight could go to the railroad company and say, "Since I give you so much freight you ought to charge me less per ton than if I shipped only a little." In many cases the railroad felt that it had to agree. The usual arrangement was for the shipper to pay the regular freight

rate; but at the end of the month, or at some other specified time, the railroad would give back part of it. This was called a rebate. Rebates meant that the big shippers got steadily richer and bigger, while small shippers grew smaller and poorer.

That led to worse things. When a state legislature seemed about to pass a law forbidding something that the railroads were doing, the railroad men and the big shippers would get together and secretly pay some of the legislators money to vote against the bill. That was bribery and was against the law, even then, but who was going to tell about it? Not the men who gave the bribes nor those who took them, you may be sure. Honest men knew what was going on, but often they couldn't prove it. Sometimes judges were actually bribed to give the wrong decision in court.

Railroad rebates were only one of many kinds of dirty work that went on in the wild scramble to make money. Oil was becoming more important, not only for lamps, but also to keep machines running smoothly, and the number of machines was increasing rapidly. Then, in 1876, a German named Nikolaus Otto invented an engine that could be driven by exploding a mixture of air and gasoline inside a cylinder, instead of using steam; so oil, from which gasoline is made, became really important.

Soon so many oil wells were drilled that there was too much oil on the market and the price fell very low. Then John D. Rockefeller organized most of the oil refiners and dealers into one company, the Standard Oil Company, which by the help of rebates and other means drove nearly everybody else out of the oil business. The Standard Oil Company could charge whatever it pleased, since you could hardly get oil anywhere else, and Rockefeller became the richest man in the country and perhaps in the entire world.

The same kind of thing happened in the steel industry, except that it was not a steelmaker who organized it, but a banker, John Pierpont Morgan. He, too, became immensely rich and immensely powerful. When one man, or one company, has all the oil there is, or all the steel or all of anything else that people need, it is called a monopoly. In the old days monarchs used to grant monopolies to their favorites. For instance, Elizabeth the Great, Queen of England, gave the Earl of Essex a monopoly on sweet wines from Spain and Portugal, so that no one else could sell them in England. It made the earl very rich but it made the people very angry, so at last Parliament passed a law which forbade the giving of monopolies.

There was no law preventing a man from going

141

out and getting a monopoly for himself, either by making deals with his rivals or by driving them out of business. So this practice went on freely in our country. Not only oil and steel, but sugar, tobacco, meat packing, and many other industries were organized into huge combinations. Men like Rockefeller and Morgan always claimed that they did not have a real monopoly, that there were always others engaged in the same business. But the others were so small that they counted for little.

These men had another scheme for avoiding the accusation of holding monopolies. Instead of buying five or six — or fifty or sixty — companies and combining them into one, they made an agreement whereby each owner handed over the stock in his company to a small group of men who then managed all the stock. These men did not own it. They merely held it, as the law says, "in trust" for the owners, and they turned the profits over to the owners. These groups were the trusts, which in most people's minds came to mean, before long, the same thing as monopolies.

At first the trusts were looked on as a fine idea and the men who organized them were given the rather fancy title of captains of industry. But as time passed it became plain that one thing they did was to give a few men power to drive everybody else out of the trust-controlled business, and after that they could charge any price they pleased. So people changed their minds about the men who ran the trusts; instead of admiring them, they began to hate them, and instead of naming them captains of industry, years later President Theodore Roosevelt called them "malefactors of great wealth." A malefactor is an evildoer, so this put the industrialists in the same class as criminals.

This was a pretty bad period in the history of the United States. Nobody can deny it and today not many people try to deny it. One historian, Claude G. Bowers, has called it *The Tragic Era,* which implies that it was sad as well as bad. Not many people will deny that, either.

The people who suffered most were the farmers and the factory workers. Every time there was a financial panic — and the clumsy money system brought on great panics in 1873, 1893, and 1907 — farmers and other people who worked with their hands came near to starving. In about 1890 they began to combine to see if they couldn't get better laws. They formed a third party which they called the People's Party; its members were known as Populists. They elected a number of congressmen and senators, especially in the West and South; but they didn't get very far until they joined — *fused* was what they called it

— with the Democratic party in 1896. Then in a tremendous campaign they came very near electing the Democratic candidate for president — William Jennings Bryan, a lawyer from Nebraska, and the finest American orator since Daniel Webster. (Lincoln can't be counted, for he was more than an orator and his speeches were true philosophy, not mere eloquence.) However, William McKinley, the Republican candidate, was elected by a narrow margin and nothing was done about the trusts.

It was far from true, of course, that everybody connected with a trust was wicked. Such men as Rockefeller and Morgan, for example, were at one time regarded as not much better than the devil himself, but as a matter of fact they had many good qualities. To begin with, the kerosene that Rockefeller's company turned out was good kerosene, and he organized a system to deliver it that worked so well that you could buy it practically anywhere in the world, even far in the interior of China. Morgan's steel was good steel, and though the steel trust charged plenty for it, it never charged so much that people were reluctant to use it. So it was with most of the other trust-made goods. The price was high, but the quality was usually good and you could always get them quickly and easily.

Sometimes, it is true, the trusts not only charged

high prices but delivered bad goods. During the war with Spain in 1898 there was a great scandal because the meat packers were selling the army spoiled meat; and a few years later — in 1906 — a novelist, Upton Sinclair, found and wrote about such filthy conditions in the packing houses that President Theodore Roosevelt ordered an investigation which led to the pure-food laws.

But most of the things turned out at this time were well made, and the big companies were usually quick to snatch up any new invention and put it on the market. It was during this period that Thomas A. Edison invented the electric light, the talking machine, and the moving picture. Many men, here and in Europe, were trying to mount Otto's gasoline engine on a carriage. Shortly before 1900 they began to succeed in a big way, and we got the automobile.

Most of the Americans who made vast fortunes, however unfairly, were a long way from being nothing but greedy money grabbers. A few were just that, but not many. Rockefeller and Morgan were great churchgoers; Rockefeller was a deacon in the Baptist Church, Morgan a vestryman in the Episcopal Church. Both felt that a man who has made a great deal of money ought to put it to some public use. Rockefeller, during his life (he lived to

be ninety-six), gave the greater part of his money to colleges, universities, hospitals, medical schools, and other public institutions. Morgan was interested in art, and he bought, brought to this country, and later gave to museums and art galleries, a great many beautiful things, some of them made by the greatest artists who ever lived. He also bought rare books and manuscripts and built a library in New York where American scholars are allowed to study them.

Andrew Carnegie, who came from Scotland as an immigrant boy and became one of the great steel men, offered to build a public library for any American town that would agree to support it, and built thousands of them. He gave 7500 pipe organs to churches and set up half a dozen scientific and educational institutions; but he is best remembered for having said that any rich American who dies without having given largely to public institutions "dies disgraced." In no other country have so many of the richest men agreed with him.

It must be remembered, too, that most of these men never violated the law. The trouble was that the law, as it then stood, did not protect the public interest. It had never before been necessary to protect it in that way, for never before had so much power been gathered into the hands of a few men.

It seems to be a fact that the country was so strong and vigorous at this time that nothing could hurt it much, not even the work of men who were bad through and through. Perhaps the worst political leader we ever had was William Marcy Tweed, of New York. He got together unscrupulous men, and through them organized the ignorant people, especially the many thousands who had just come to this country and knew nothing of American ways. By means of these people he elected members of his gang as mayor and other officers of the city, and they stole millions. But at last the law caught up with him and he died in jail.

Tweed was a scoundrel, through and through. It is doubtful that he ever intentionally did one thing for the public good. But one of his ways of stealing was to build something, a road or a bridge or a courthouse, charge the city two or three times what it cost, and put the difference in his own pocket and in the pockets of his gang. He did this sort of thing with Central Park in New York City, which up to that time had been nothing but vacant land. Tweed made drives and footpaths and bridges and ornamental ponds all through the place; and although he got a great deal of dishonest money out of it, the city got a beautiful park. It is probably true that Central Park today is worth more than all that the

Tweed gang stole. So even the villains couldn't hurt the United States very much.

On the other hand, many of the men who built the trusts also built fine and valuable things. Two of the very early millionaires, Johns Hopkins and Ezra Cornell, used part of their money to endow universities; and, later, so did Rockefeller, Vanderbilt, Stanford, Duke, and others. Many established what are called foundations; that is, they put their money in the hands of trustees to be used for some good purpose, perhaps to advance education or science or public health or religion or aid for the afflicted.

So many of them did that kind of thing that perhaps they added something to Americanism. In most other countries that are not Communist, people pretty generally agree that a man's money is his own and he can do with it anything he likes. Americans usually think that Carnegie was right, and that a man with a very large fortune who doesn't give a big part of it to something for the public good is a low kind of fellow, really not fit to be called an American. We know that a man who plays the game strictly according to the rules can make a lot of money in America. But if he gets a very great amount — hundreds of millions — we feel the chances are that in some way the rules were rigged

and he didn't really make all that money, the
country made it for him; so for him to give a great
deal of it back to the country is no more than right.

Since the Industrial Revolution large fortunes
have been made everywhere; and as the large fortunes grew, all the world learned that wealth means
power. Now when one man gains great power, many
other men are not going to like it. Usually they get
together to do something about it. So in every
country in the world you will find a party, or perhaps a group too small to be called a party, who
think it is dangerous to leave so much power in the
hands of private citizens. There are many different
ideas as to what ought to be done about it. In general, liberals are inclined to think that if the right
kind of laws are enacted, there will not be much
danger that the poor will be oppressed and robbed
by the rich. Socialists go farther. They think that the
government had better take charge of most of the
things that produce wealth — land, factories, railroads, and so on. Communists go farthest of all.
They say that all power should be held by the government, and that everyone should be made to do
what is good for the country, whether he likes it or
not.

You might think that where the private fortunes
are greatest, the dislike of the rich will be strongest

and these parties of protest will be largest. You would then expect the United States to be a Communist country, or at least a country with a very large Communist party. But the truth is exactly the opposite. The United States, with more great private fortunes than any other big country, is the least Communist of all of them. For that matter, the Socialist party here has always been small, and the country is not even liberal all the time.

We have found that while a man with many millions has power to do a lot of harm, he also has power to do a lot of good, and we are apt to think that the good is greater than the harm. We got that idea from the great millionaires themselves, especially those who made their money in the years after the Civil War, and who showed how much good a man with a great fortune could do. This has made us pretty careful about enacting laws to cut down the fortunes — so careful that we are now regarded as the most conservative self-governing people in the world.

Our most severe law against wealth is the income tax. Everybody has to pay some tax, and the tax increases as the income gets bigger until, if a man makes more than $300,000 a year, he has to pay nine tenths of everything above that in income taxes.

The truth at the bottom of this is that most Americans just don't believe that any man's work is worth a thousand dollars a day. If he is getting that much, he is getting part of what somebody else has earned. He may be doing it lawfully, but he isn't doing it by his own efforts; so if he is taxed nine tenths of it, he is still getting a tenth that he didn't earn.

At that, some Americans are still piling up big fortunes, because the government does not take away what a man already has, and often what he has increases in value. But most people don't worry about big fortunes, because so far they can't see that the fortunes have done us any great harm, and some of them have been put to very good uses. There is no doubt that this feeling was built up in part by such men as Carnegie and Rockefeller and others who made their money by means that were lawful then, but very questionable now; having made it, they used it for good.

It is really hard to give one name to the period after the Civil War. It was shameful, but not all shameful. It tore down some things, but it built up others. And it did more than all the fighting to make the typical American the kind of man he is today.

CHAPTER NINE

Rough Rider in the White House

HISTORY flows on like a river. You can't chop it into segments, saying, "On such and such a day this piece ended and the next piece began." It doesn't happen that way. One era merges into another as smoothly and easily as a river swings around a wide bend. You can stand on the bank of a river at one place and say without the slightest doubt, "Here it is flowing south." Then you can walk along it for maybe half a mile to another place and say just as positively, "Here it is flowing west." But you can't pick any point between and say, "Here it quit flowing south and started flowing west," because it swings gently around a long curve. You can tell about where it happened, but not exactly.

It is the same way with history. You can say that

153

the United States was going in a certain direction in 1890. You can say that it was going in another direction in 1910. But nobody knows the exact moment when it changed. Yet change it did, and for convenience we usually say that it changed about 1900.

The Republican party won the presidential election in 1896 and it managed to hold on to power in 1900, but the wiser Republicans saw that they couldn't go on in the old way. They would have to do something about the big business combines that had power enough to rob everybody.

One of the sharpest minds in the party was that of the man who had been elected vice-president in 1900 when McKinley was re-elected to a second term as president. His name was Theodore Roosevelt and he belonged to a New York family that was fairly rich, although nothing like the Rockefellers and Morgans. As a boy, Theodore had asthma and was rather spindly, so he was sent out West to see if fresh air and sunshine would improve his health. They did. Living outdoors, much of the time on a horse, herding cattle, riding the range, and in his spare time hunting everything from wolves and grizzly bears to cattle thieves, Roosevelt became sturdy and active. More than that, he had a fine time, fell in love with the West, and made a great number of friends among the Western people. But after a few years he came back to New York.

Then in 1898 we had a war with Spain — a small war, because Spain was in no condition to fight, but the most exciting thing that had happened to the country since 1865. Roosevelt rushed back to the West and among his cowboy friends raised a regiment of cavalry in which every man was a splendid horseman. Their official name was First Volunteer Cavalry, but they called themselves the Rough Riders. The colonel was a former Army doctor named Leonard Wood; Roosevelt was the lieutenant colonel and he became colonel when Wood was promoted to brigadier general. In an attack on San Juan Hill, in Cuba, Colonel Roosevelt distinguished himself and came back a national hero. So in 1900 the Republicans nominated Roosevelt for vice-president, although the old politicians in the party didn't like him much.

Then in 1901 a crazy anarchist shot McKinley, and Roosevelt became president. (Anarchists are people who believe, or say that they believe, that all government is wrong and that there should be none.) At once Roosevelt set to work to bring the trusts under the rule of law, and he quickly became the most popular politician in America. He did some other good things, too, but no one man could change the whole system, and Roosevelt was slowed down because half his own party was satisfied with things as they were and worked against him. But he started a great many things, and it cannot be denied that he did much to make people more important than money in the American system.

Yet it was not entirely because he was a good president that people liked Theodore Roosevelt. He was a likeable man. He was hearty, full of life, fond of games, a good boxer and a better wrestler, a wonderful cross-country hiker, and at the same time interested in learning, especially in science and history. He wrote many books, and as president he invited to the White House kinds of people that few

presidents since Jefferson had cared to have around
— artists, musicians, inventors, explorers, poets, and
philosophers. In his time you found at the White
House more brilliant and learned men than you could
find anywhere else in Washington; yet among them
you were also likely to find a cowboy or a champion
prize fighter or a top tennis player. Roosevelt was
interested in everybody, so everybody was interested
in him, and even those who laughed at the excitement he stirred up rather liked him. At least he was
not dull.

The word usually used to describe Theodore
Roosevelt is *progressive,* which he was, in a way;
yet in another way he might be called regressive,

which is just the opposite. That is to say, he helped turn the country back to the old idea — the idea held by Washington, Jefferson, Jackson, and Lincoln — that a good president must feel responsible for any great national problem.

The presidents between Lincoln and Roosevelt were Johnson, Grant, Hayes, Garfield, Arthur (he was elected vice-president and became president when Garfield was murdered), Cleveland, Harrison (this was Benjamin Harrison, a grandson of W. H. Harrison, who had been president back in 1840), Cleveland again, and McKinley. Except for Cleveland there wasn't a real leader in the whole bunch, and Cleveland's main work was simply to clean out the rascals and put honest men in government jobs.

If any of these presidents — always excepting Cleveland — thought much about any great national problem, it was the problem of pulling the country together after the damage caused by the Civil War. However, the railroad and the telegraph actually were pulling the country together. When it became possible for businessmen in cities as far apart as New York and New Orleans to trade easily with profit to both, then there was no longer any sense in pulling apart. Until the railroad came, it was easier for both cities to trade with London than with each other; for they could send their goods to London and bring back British goods by water in less time and with less danger than by sailing along the coast, around Florida, and across the Gulf of Mexico.

As for the West, there was no Panama Canal, and it was necessary to go around the tip of South America at Cape Horn — a stormy, terrible place for sailing ships — to get to California. When a railroad was built across the continent, California became, you could almost say, next door to the other states.

So the United States grew together very rapidly from 1865 to 1900, and about the best that can be said for the presidents during that time is that they mildly approved of the process and did nothing to hinder it. The fact is, that although they could see what was going on they had little, if any, idea of what it meant, as far as government was concerned. Apparently they didn't think it meant anything in particular. They certainly didn't think it meant that they should step in and lead the way to forming a government better suited to the solid, compact country that America was becoming.

They excused themselves by quoting a saying of Thomas Jefferson. When he looked around him he saw a huge, sprawling country, thickly settled only in spots, which were separated by wide stretches of almost empty land. The thickly settled spots had different kinds of soil, which grew different kinds of crops, under different kinds of weather, with different kinds of people; and they really had little to do with each other. Never dreaming of a railroad or a telegraph, Jefferson thought that the United States must remain that way, probably for two hundred and fifty years. So he decided, as any man of sense would have decided, that the best thing the central government could do was to let each community develop in its own way, with no more interference from Washington than was absolutely necessary. And this came to be expressed in a maxim: "That government is best which governs least."

But few things that were true of this country in 1801, when Jefferson became president, were still true in 1901, when Theodore Roosevelt became president. For one thing, Jefferson was president of five million people, Roosevelt of seventy-five million. What was more important, in 1901 when the president said anything important in Washington, it was known in New Orleans, San Francisco, New York, and Boston in a matter of minutes. There was no radio yet, and they didn't get telephone lines all the way to San Francisco until 1915, so the people in other cities couldn't hear his voice, but the telegraph told them what he said; and that alone was enough to make government a different thing from what it had been in Jefferson's time.

Some people paid attention to this change. Wise men all over the country had been thinking about it for years, and some of them got into the House of Representatives and the Senate. But Roosevelt was the first president who understood it. When he came to the White House, those senators and representatives who really knew what was going on and were trying to get the laws changed to fit the new kind of country found that they had a leader.

Most of these men were from the states in the Mississippi Valley. That was a great farming region and the Populist movement of ten years earlier had shaken things up at a great rate in that region. Others came from large cities, where the factory workers felt that they were not getting a fair deal. In some places it was regarded as a crime to join a labor union, and in many places when union men tried to strike for higher wages or shorter hours or anything else, the police stopped their meetings, beat the strikers, threw them into jail, and occasionally even shot them down.

So when Roosevelt announced that he proposed to break up the trusts and give farmers and labor their rights, a great many party leaders were ready to help him. So were some Democrats, in spite of the fact that Roosevelt was a Republican; but at this time the Democratic party was so weak that it didn't amount to much. Cleveland was the only president it had elected since the Civil War, and it didn't have many members of Congress.

The big fight was within the Republican party — the Progressives, as Roosevelt's followers were called, against those who were satisfied with things as they were. Under Roosevelt's leadership the Progressives passed a number of laws to stop unfair business practices, and the President saw to it that the Department of Justice enforced them. Of course this meant that Roosevelt stepped on a good many people's toes and they didn't like it. They called him a wild radical. They said he was trying to become a dictator. They accused him of violating the Constitution and setting up a tyranny. More than one crackpot tried to kill him, but we had at last learned to keep guards around the president, and the lunatics were stopped before they could reach him.

But Roosevelt saw beyond what was going on here in America. He realized that the United States was becoming one of the Great Powers, as the biggest and strongest nations of the world were then called. He tried to make the American people realize it, and with some success but not very much. He persuaded Congress to strengthen the Army, and especially the Navy. One of his last acts as president was to send the battle fleet on a cruise around the world,

partly to stir up American pride in the Navy and partly as a warning to other nations.

Theodore Roosevelt was highhanded. His best friends cannot deny it. Most of the time he was right, but once in a while he was in such a rush that he did unwise and even unjust things. Yet of all his highhanded acts, the one that looked worst turned out to be of great value to this country and to the rest of the world. This was the way he got the Panama Canal started.

The Isthmus of Panama at that time was part of the republic of Colombia. Many years earlier a French company bought from Colombia the right to dig a canal across the isthmus, but they couldn't manage to do it and went broke, mainly because

yellow fever and malaria killed off too many of their workers. So the United States bought the French rights, paying $40,000,000 to the stockholders. Then, to make things all legal and correct, we offered to make a treaty with Colombia and to pay her $15,000,000 merely to confirm the rights. At first the Colombians agreed and everything seemed to be all right; but at the last minute they refused to sign the treaty until they got more money.

To Roosevelt this looked like a plain holdup, and he was indignant. So were the French, because they couldn't get their money until the deal was complete. So were the storekeepers and hotelkeepers and so on in Panama, for they hoped to make a lot of money

when thousands of workmen came in to build the canal, and afterward when ships began to pass through it. The French and the businessmen and politicians in Panama got together and decided to do something about it. They put on a revolution, declared the province of Panama independent of Colombia, and offered to sign the canal treaty.

Roosevelt instantly declared that Panama was now an independent country and sent several United States warships there "to preserve order," as he said, but really to prevent the Colombians from putting down the revolution. Colombia couldn't fight the United States, so she had to give in.

The canal was started with private contractors doing the work, but they didn't get very far, so in 1906 Roosevelt put the whole thing under the War Department. First they sent down an Army doctor, Colonel Gorgas, and he cleaned up the place so well that yellow fever and malaria practically disappeared. Then they sent down an Army engineer, Lieutenant Colonel Goethals, and in eight years he had the canal built. It was opened in August, 1914, just as World War I was breaking out in Europe.

This was lucky for us, because it enabled the United States Navy to move quickly from one side of the country to the other without going all the way around South America.

Roosevelt may have been wrong in the way he did it, but what he did in Panama helped the country. Even those men who wish that he had been a little more careful in the way he went about it can't blame him very much and can't regret what he accomplished. After all, we got the canal, and if he had not started it when he did we should not have had it during World War I, when it was badly needed. So it was with a good many other things. Roosevelt was rough in his methods, but he was usually right in what he was trying to do. The country owes him a great deal.

Yet neither the Panama Canal nor the trust busting nor any of the other exciting things that happened at this time had as much effect in making Americans what they are as did the way Roosevelt made them think about the president. He made us think about him the way people used to think about Andrew Jackson and as they had thought about no other president since. This includes Lincoln, for Lincoln was president during a great war, and everybody admits that in wartime a president must lead.

Jackson and Roosevelt led in time of peace. Washington did, too, but Washington was not quite like any other president. He was the one man whom everybody trusted, so he was more like a great umpire than anything else. He was on nobody's side. He was there to see that everybody obeyed the rules. Jefferson was frankly on one side. He was on the side of the people at home and against the people who held government jobs. But Jackson was on the side of the common people, not only against government job holders but also against the rich and powerful men outside the government. So was Roosevelt.

This got the people back into the habit of thinking of the president as in a special way their man. They thought about Roosevelt as they had never thought about the respectable but dull and slow-moving gentlemen who had held the office since Lincoln.

This really added something to the American character — yet perhaps *added* is not the right word. Maybe it is better to say that this restored something that had been lost since Jackson's time. That something is the idea of the president as a leader. He is not a good president if he is content to sit still and let other people think up all the new ideas. He should get out and start something on his own account. He is sworn to defend the Constitution, but the modern American thinks that is not enough. He should also make the Constitution effective, make it work, make it do what the preamble says it should do; that is, "secure the blessings of liberty to ourselves and our posterity."

CHAPTER TEN

Professor in Politics

TO SOME people Theodore Roosevelt seemed, like Tigger in the A. A. Milne stories, "too bouncy." It is true that to the end of his life there was something boyish in him, a sort of helter-skelter quality that made him successful at getting things done but not so good at sitting down and thinking out carefully what the consequences would be.

He was very much a man of his time, for the truth is that during the early years of the present century the whole country was too bouncy. It was very much like a boy who is just growing into a man. He usually feels that it is fine to be old enough to manage his own affairs without having to consult anyone about every little thing he does. And it *is* fine; freedom is one of the finest things in the world. But very soon that boy is going to find out that freedom is not all that manhood brings him. With freedom, he gets responsibility. There are things that people will pass by when they are done by a small boy, but will not tolerate when they are done by a young man. They say, "He is old enough to know better," and call for a policeman.

Nations, too, are like that when they have gained freedom and then begin to gain power. They are eager to do what they want to do, but they are slow to believe that there are things they must do even though some of them are unpleasant. Boys who have good stuff in them gradually face up to their responsibilities as they turn into young men, and it is the same way with nations. It is a part of growing up. Yet since a nation lives many times longer than a man, it is not surprising that what a boy usually does in a year or two may take a nation a decade or two, or even longer.

By 1900 — in fact, by about 1893 — nearly all the good land between the Atlantic and the Pacific had people living on it. In 1864 Congress had passed a law giving any soldier who had fought two years the right to go into the West, pick out any 160 acres of public land that suited him, and live on it for a year, after which it would be his. This was called the Homestead Law. Later anybody was allowed to gain a homestead by living on it five years and paying a small fee. Anybody who would build a railroad across the public land was given part of the land on both sides of the track, and this land he could sell to settlers. All this was intended to help fill the country with people, and it worked.

Some land had been kept by the government — "withdrawn from settlement" was the term — for future use. Theodore Roosevelt was especially active in this. He set aside some land that was covered with fine timber and some that was known to contain valuable minerals; some where the scenery was especially beautiful he made into national parks, which anybody can enjoy but nobody can own. The national parks belong to all the people. The Yellowstone and Glacier National Parks in the West and the Great Smoky National Park in the East were selected for their beauty, the Grand Canyon and the Wind Cave National Parks because of their curious formations, and the Mesa Verde Park because of its ancient Indian relics. There are twenty-nine of these national parks besides many smaller historical parks and national monuments.

But except for the parks and some areas which were uninhabitable for various reasons, it is true to say that the country was all settled by the year 1900. It was like a boy who, by the time he is seventeen, has grown as tall as he will ever be. He will fill out, of course, and grow much heavier and much stronger, but he has, as people say, gained his height. Fifty years after 1900 the United States had almost twice as many people, but no more land. It had filled out and grown stronger, but it had not stretched in area.

Yet it was not really a full-grown nation, even under Theodore Roosevelt. Having easily won the war with Spain in 1898, it had become pretty cocky. Wise men knew that Spain was an old broken-down kingdom that couldn't put up much of a fight; other men didn't think of that. They remembered only that Spain had once been a Great Power — for a time the greatest in the world — so because we had defeated her, they acted as if they thought we could defeat any nation. For a while we carried on as if our word were law and everybody else had to stand out of our way.

But that mood didn't last long. Soon we found that growing up brings plenty of trouble with it. In 1898 we made Spain give up Cuba, Puerto Rico, and the Philippine Islands because she had been misgoverning them all terribly. Cuba we set free, and Puerto Rico we arranged to protect, but what we were to do with the Philippine Islands nobody knew. In fact, we didn't know exactly why we had taken them in the first place, since they were on the other side of the world. But there had been a Spanish fleet in

Manila harbor when the war broke out, and Commodore George Dewey, commanding our Asiatic squadron at Hong Kong, was ordered to go in and sink it, which he did.

Incidentally, that was a very curious battle. Only one of Dewey's men was killed and only eight were wounded. The Spaniards had 167 killed and 214 wounded, besides having all their ships sunk. The fight began at 5 a.m. and at 7:35 a. m. the American ships ceased fire and the Spaniards sent cablegrams saying they had won. But soon the Americans opened up again and finished the Spanish fleet. The story spread around that Dewey had stopped fighting in order that his men might eat breakfast — which, in fact, they did — but the real reason was to check on his ammunition, which some excited officer had told him was running low, although actually there was plenty.

So now the Navy was in possession of Manila Bay and there was nothing to do but send an army to take the city. We found, however, that we had a very hot potato. Although the Spaniards gave us little trouble (in fact, they seemed glad to get out), we found that the islands were torn by a quarrel that had been going on for centuries between the pagan Moros, some of whom were downright savages, and the Filipinos, who were Christians and pretty well civilized but had never been able to put down the Moros. It seemed very likely that, if we simply left the island, either the Moros, who were first-rate fighters, would come in and exterminate the Filipinos, or the Filipinos would wipe out the Moros. In either case a lot of people were sure to be killed, and most of the property in the island might be destroyed; and we didn't want to be responsible for such a disaster.

The final outcome was that we stayed in the islands for more than forty years and had rather an unhappy time there. For several years it was very unhappy, for first the Moros and then the Filipinos turned on us. They were glad to get rid of the Spaniards, but they had no wish to be ruled by Americans. First we went after the Moros and the fighting was hot and heavy for a while; but at last they were ambushed and completely conquered by an officer that nobody but Army people had ever heard of up to that time. He was Major John J. Pershing. Theodore Roosevelt was so pleased that he jumped him from major to brigadier general at once, without the usual intermediate steps. It made a lot of colonels very sore, but it was a good idea, as we found out fifteen years later when World War I came along.

No sooner had we dealt with the Moros than the

Filipinos rose under a man named Emilio Aguinaldo, who proved to be a skillful fighter and gave us plenty of trouble for more than two years. But at last General Frederick Funston, with only a handful of men, made a daring raid behind the lines and captured Aguinaldo. After that, the rebellion soon petered out. In later years Aguinaldo became a good friend of the United States and gave us much help in keeping peace in the islands.

Then, in 1900, a secret society of Chinese fanatics calling themselves Boxers, undertook to butcher all the foreigners in China, and did murder a number. Most of the foreigners in Peking got into the British legation, where they were besieged all summer. Various nations, including the United States, sent a combined army that finally got the people out. One of the Americans who helped defend the legation in Peking was Herbert Hoover, who later became President of the United States.

In 1904, Russia and Japan went to war over Manchuria, which belonged to neither of them, but to China. There was danger that the winner would take over all of China. Japan won a great sea battle and two battles on land, but they left her depleted and Russia was bringing up vast new armies; so when President Roosevelt stepped in as peacemaker both sides agreed on terms to end the war. Japan got Manchuria, but she didn't get the rest of China.

In 1906, there was an uproar on the other side of the world. Germany seemed about to fight France and Great Britain, to decide who should have Morocco, in North Africa. President Roosevelt intervened again and persuaded all hands to meet in a conference at Algeciras, where things were smoothed over for the time being.

All this meant that whenever serious trouble broke out in any part of the world the United States, having become one of the Great Powers, was expected to help calm the excited adversaries before they started a war. We were feeling the responsibilities of a grown-up nation, and many Americans didn't like

it at all. When the treaty of Algeciras came before the Senate, the senators ratified it; but they attached a clause saying that this didn't mean that the United States intended to play any part in European affairs. That was a slap at Roosevelt, for it practically said that he had stepped into Europe's concerns without any real reason for doing so.

The truth is, he was trying to prevent the outbreak of a European war, which he knew would involve us. The senators were acting like small boys, refusing to accept the responsibility that the size and power of the United States had brought upon it. Whether the Senate liked it or not, troubles continued to multiply, and soon they were a great deal

closer home than places like China and Morocco.

When Roosevelt left the presidency in 1909 he was succeeded by William H. Taft. We have never had a more honest president than Taft, but we have seldom had one less fit to lead the country at a time when things were changing rapidly and nobody knew exactly what to do. Taft couldn't even lead his own party, much less the country. He was no sooner in the White House than the progressive and the conservative Republicans began to fight each other, and it was not long before the conservatives won the president over to their side.

This crowd was not so much corrupt as stupid. They couldn't see why it was impossible to run this country in 1909 the way Alexander Hamilton wanted to run it in 1800. Hamilton said that the most important thing was to get the rich lined up behind the government, because if the rich men backed it, the poor could never tear it down. If there had ever been a time when Hamilton was right, that time was past long before 1909. Yet Taft appointed as Secretary of the Interior a man named Ballinger, who believed in Hamilton's ideas.

The Secretary of the Interior had charge of Alaska, which was then a territory. Nearly all the land still belonged to the government, and Roosevelt had been in favor of keeping most of this land until it could be used to good advantage by the government. Some of it, however, had coal under it, and a big coal-mining man named Cunningham decided that the coal was worth a lot of money, and he filed claims for that part of the land. Ballinger, true to the principle of making it worthwhile for rich men to support the government, let the Cunningham claims go through.

This made the Progressives furious. Theodore Roosevelt had gone hunting in Africa, but his friends raised a tremendous hullabaloo, and when Roosevelt heard of what was going on he was as angry as any of them.

For a while there was a first-class scandal, for some of the Progressives believed, and did not hesitate to say, that Ballinger was a crook who had been bribed by Cunningham. An investigation showed that was not true. Ballinger simply believed that he was doing the right thing in turning over public land to men who would get out the coal or the timber or whatever else might be of value. If the government helped rich men make more money, that would make the rich men more strongly in favor of the government, and Ballinger could see nothing wrong in that.

Theodore Roosevelt and his friends saw plenty that was wrong in it. Roosevelt had been strongly in favor of the election of Taft, thinking that Taft would carry on the Roosevelt policies. Now he felt that Taft had double-crossed him. So when he got back from his hunting trip he announced that the Republican party must not nominate Taft for a second term; and when the party paid no attention to him — by this time it was controlled by the conservatives — Roosevelt organized what he called the Progressive party, and ran against both Taft and the Democrats. (When he got back from Africa, newspaper reporters asked him about his health, and he said that he felt "strong as a bull moose." The expression delighted the reporters and from that time on many of them called the Progressives the Bull Moose Party.)

The Democrats nominated Woodrow Wilson in 1912. At the election in November, Taft got three million votes; Roosevelt got four million; but Wilson, the Democrat, got six million and became president.

The election of Woodrow Wilson is a very important date in American history, partly because of the kind of man he was, but still more because of the way things were going in this country and in the rest of the world when he became president.

If you think of the current of events as flowing along like a river, then you can say that the river of American history had been swinging around a great bend ever since the war with Spain in 1898. How-

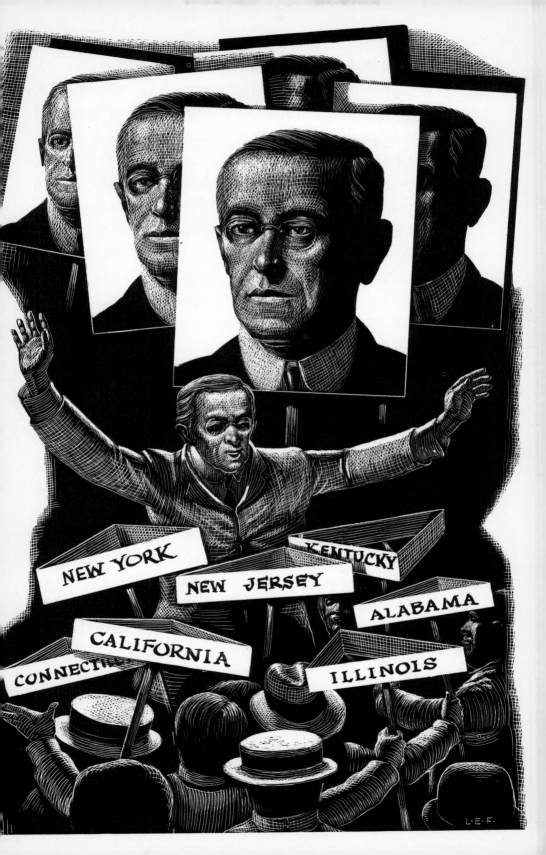

ever, when we get to the election of Wilson, in 1912, we can say definitely that it had already turned and was flowing in a different direction.

From Washington's presidency through McKinley's we were gradually becoming a nation with many responsibilities toward its own people. About the time of Theodore Roosevelt, we finally became one. Then we began to move toward becoming a Great Power, with many responsibilities toward other nations, as well as to our own people.

All this was clearly understood by the man that the Democrats elected President in 1912. He was not a politician in the ordinary sense. He had been a university president and then a governor. It astonished many people, when Woodrow Wilson left Princeton University and became Governor of New Jersey, that he knew so much about managing a state. They forgot that the president of an American university has to learn a lot about managing people if he is to run his university as it should be run; and university professors as a rule are not easy people to manage. At any rate, Wilson did so well in New Jersey that he attracted attention all over the country; so the Democratic party decided that he would be a good man to run against Roosevelt and Taft, when the Republican party split.

The party was right. How right it was most Democrats never dreamed at the time; in fact, we are not sure even yet, because many of the things that Wilson started have not yet been worked out and after nearly fifty years we are not certain whether they will succeed or fail. He was a great man who played a part in great events, and many years must pass before anybody can evaluate such a man.

Theodore Roosevelt had been a well-educated man and an excellent writer. Wilson was much more the intellectual type, and when it came to explaining what the government was doing and why, he was one of the great writers of the century. He had faults, of course. While he was trying to decide some question he would listen carefully to anybody with ideas and frequently would accept them; but once he had made up his mind he was one of the stubbornest men who ever lived. Then when men opposed something that Wilson felt sure was right, it was hard for him to believe that they were honestly mistaken. He was likely to decide that they were wicked, and begin to hate them.

But Wilson was honest, he was brave, and he had studied history for many years. He knew far better than most men exactly how this country had grown, and also how others which, like the United States, had begun small and weak, had later grown great, and then weakened and gone down. He was sure that he knew the mistakes they had made, and he was determined to do all he could to keep the United States from making the same mistakes.

Like Theodore Roosevelt, Wilson saw clearly that the United States was doing a good many things in ways that might have been the best possible ways at one time, but had now become silly and wrong. He said so, clearly and emphatically. The Constitution says that the president shall "from time to time give to the Congress information of the state of the Union and recommend for their consideration such measures as he shall judge necessary and expedient." This is what is known as the President's message. Washington and John Adams obeyed this order by going before Congress and saying what they had to say in person. Jefferson, who was a poor speaker and knew it, preferred to write out what he had to say and send it to Congress to be read by a clerk.

Wilson, who was a good speaker, in fact, one of the best in the world, returned to Washington's way of doing it. He went to Congress and spoke his message. It had a great effect, partly because nobody then living had ever heard a president make a speech to Congress, but mainly because he spoke beautifully and so clearly that everybody could understand exactly what he meant.

Wilson told Congress that this country was far

behind the times with regard to four particular things. One was the tariff, which was much too high. Another was the money and banking system, which was much too rigid. The third was the labor laws, which were unfair to wage earners. The fourth was the tax system, which did not make the people who had the most pay the most. Wilson asked Congress to change all of them.

All these changes that Wilson suggested were hard to work out, but the other three were easy by comparison with changing the money and banking system, and it was over this that the really terrific fight was made.

Whenever the government proposes to do anything about money, large numbers of people are sure to believe that what it proposes is all wrong and there are screams of protest. A long procession of the biggest bankers in the country went before Congress declaring that what Wilson proposed would ruin us. Some of them may have been lying to protect their own profits, but most of them were perfectly honest and believed what they said.

What Wilson proposed and what Congress finally worked out is known as the Federal Reserve System. It is an arrangement between the government and the banks "to make the currency elastic"; that is, to make the total supply of money in the country expand and contract as it is needed. For instance, in the autumn when millions of farmers are all gathering their crops at once and shipping them to market, there is need of much more money than at times when goods are not moving so rapidly.

This seems plain enough, and once the system was set up it worked so well that nobody dreams of doing away with it now. But before it was tried, shrewd businessmen really believed that Wilson was destroying property and driving the country into socialism, if not plain anarchy. Their thinking simply had not kept up with the changing times.

CHAPTER ELEVEN

America Grows Up

WOODROW WILSON was a progressive, but not with a capital "P." That is to say, he did not belong to the Bull Moose party, although his ideas were a good deal like those of Theodore Roosevelt. The main difference between the two men was that when Roosevelt discovered something wrong his first impulse was to look around for some villain who was responsible and try to put him in jail. But Wilson's first impulse, when he found something wrong, was to think out how the evildoers were getting away with it, and to change the system so that they could no longer do so.

As long as a man is president of the United States, it is pretty hard for ordinary people to understand him, because his own party is noisily insisting that he is the greatest man in the country, and the other party is just as noisily insisting that he is no good at all, which confuses us. But after he has been out of office a few years, and all the uproar centers on another man, we can usually make up our minds about him.

But forty years after Wilson left office, half the country had not yet made up its mind about him. This is because, like Franklin D. Roosevelt, he was really two presidents — a peacetime president and a war president. The two are quite different, because the chief business of a peacetime president is to be the leader of the nation, and the chief business of a war president is to be Commander in Chief of the armed forces.

In Wilson's time the presidency itself changed. It is not far wrong to say that Taft was the last man who could be president of the United States and nothing more. Since Wilson every president has also been an important — in recent years the most important — leader of all free nations. He had to be, and it made no difference whether he liked it or not.

This was because in 1914, when Wilson had been president only a little over two years, the world system of the eight Great Powers blew up in a tremendous war. By the time it was over, three of the Great Powers were smashed, three others badly damaged, and the United States was left at least the equal of the strongest power in the world. In 1913 the

Great Powers were the United States, Great Britain, France, Germany, Russia, Austria, Italy, and Japan. By 1919, when World War I had ended, Austria had vanished, Germany was defeated, Russia was torn to pieces by civil war, Great Britain, France, and Italy were badly crippled, and only the United States and Japan stood stronger than ever.

When Wilson became president, on March 4, 1913, he had no idea of what he was getting into. He believed, and most Americans believed with him, that his chief job would be to make the laws of the United States more just and helpful to citizens of the United States. As for foreign nations, he owed them nothing, except, of course, honest dealing.

But he soon found how wrong he was. The trouble in Europe had been brewing for many years, and Americans who had really studied European politics were pretty sure that war was coming. But most Americans had not been studying European politics, and the great mass of American people lacked any idea of what was going on. When the war broke out in 1914, they were so astonished that at first they couldn't believe it.

By that time, however, Wilson had learned a great deal. As soon as he became president the reports of our ambassadors and consuls began to pour in, and the foreign ambassadors in Washington began to tell him things that they wouldn't have thought of telling the newspapers. Wilson was horrified to learn that Europe was on the brink of war, but he didn't see much that he could do about it and anyhow he had plenty of foreign troubles of his own.

For one thing, Colombia was still snarling about the way Roosevelt had "taken" Panama; and Great Britain, too, felt that she had not been treated fairly. Many years before, Great Britain and this country had agreed to build what turned out to be the Panama Canal jointly, and when we decided to do it all by ourselves Great Britain gave up her claims on the understanding that the ships of all nations should be charged exactly the same toll; but when the canal was almost finished, Congress enacted a law providing that American ships might go through free. Great Britain said that was breaking our word.

On thinking it over, Wilson decided that there was some justice in what the British and the Colombians were saying, although there was a lot to be said on our side, too. But now that he had learned that war in Europe was probable, he knew that it was most important not to have any trouble about Panama, for we would need that canal badly if war did break out. So he asked Congress to give way on both points — to pay off Colombia and to charge American ships the same toll others were charged.

190

He was wildly denounced. Some said he was a weak-kneed fellow who was allowing Colombia to blackmail us. Theodore Roosevelt — he was still living and very active in 1913 — was especially indignant, because he thought the payment to Colombia was a reflection on him. Others said that in charging American ships toll for using the canal Wilson was truckling to the British and at the same time favoring the American railroads, with which the ships would compete. Wilson had to take the abuse because he couldn't mention his main reason. He knew that if the president of the United States said war was coming, that would tend to make it come faster. So he stuck to his point, and Congress finally did what he asked, on the ground that it was reasonable and right, not because we were afraid war was coming.

The Panama business was a small matter compared with the really big foreign trouble that Wilson faced. This was with Mexico. It had begun while Taft was president, but the pot didn't boil over until after Wilson had been elected.

It is a long and complicated story, and in it there is not much to be proud of on either side. On the other hand, neither was it as bad on either side as some people tried to make out. There were Mexicans who loudly asserted that the United States meant to take their country from them and make them not much better than slaves. We never meant to do anything of the kind. There were Americans who just as loudly asserted that the Mexicans were a gang of barbarians. They were, in fact, a poor but proud people who had been printing books and building universities when the United States was still unbroken wilderness inhabited only by savage Indians.

Yet the people, Mexicans and Americans alike, who said these things were not deliberate liars; they really believed what they said and that was at the bottom of the trouble. Neither nation understood what the other was trying to do.

What Americans failed to allow for was that Mexico, the rest of Central America, and all of South America had been handled much more roughly under Spanish rule — in the case of Brazil under Portuguese rule — than we had been under British rule. So when we broke away from the king of England, we were better equipped to set up a system of self-government that would work than the Mexicans were when they broke away from the king of Spain. They had to learn immediately what our ancestors had been studying for centuries.

The Mexicans of course remembered the war of 1846, in which they had been badly defeated, and they did not love us for that. Who would? But worse came after that war. In trying to make democracy work, the Mexicans fell into error after error and for thirty years there had hardly been anything that deserved to be called a government in the country. At last, in 1877, a very hard character named Porfirio Diaz, half Spanish, half Indian, gained control and, except for one short interval, stayed in power until 1911. He abolished liberty, but he did establish law in Mexico. The country became peaceful, because Diaz promptly shot anybody who raised a disturbance, regardless of whether the disturber was right or wrong.

Now Mexico, although poor in farm land, has many rich mines and oil fields. Soon Americans began to go down there to make something of both. They found it easy to deal with Diaz; just give him a share of the profits, and they could do pretty much what they pleased with the mines and oil wells.

It was a pretty raw deal, but the Americans excused themselves by saying that Diaz, after all, was the government of Mexico and the only one, so they had to deal with him. They made large profits, but they were careful to pay Diaz his share, exactly as they had agreed; as for what he did with the money, that was not their affair. Besides, they were giving a great many Mexicans jobs in their mines and oil fields, so the Mexicans were really better off than they were before the Americans came.

But look at it from the Mexicans' side. A great many of them saw Diaz as a bloody and cruel tyrant. The Americans were giving that man millions of dollars with which he hired soldiers to shoot down anybody who dared oppose what he was doing. Therefore Diaz was the Americans' man, and they were responsible for what he did, which made the Americans enemies of the Mexican people. So hatred between the two nations kept piling up, although most of it was due to misunderstanding, rather than real wickedness.

Finally Francisco Madero organized a revolt, defeated Diaz' army, and threw the dictator out. This was in 1911, while Taft was president. Madero was an honest man, but he shared the feeling of the rest of the Mexicans, and he got tough with the American oil men and mine owners. They ran to Washington, screaming that they were being robbed. Taft was not at all sure just who was being robbed, and he refused to send the American Army to put down Madero. But there were plenty of Mexicans willing to undertake the job, especially Huerta, a general in the Mexican Army, and about as nasty a character as the United States ever had to deal with until Hitler came along. Huerta's gang started a riot in

Mexico City, captured Madero, and shot him while, as they said, he was trying to escape. Few Americans believed he was trying to escape; they were sure it was cold-blooded murder.

This happened in February, 1913, just at the end of Taft's term; and that was the situation that confronted Wilson when he became president in March. He didn't handle it any too well. After all, Woodrow Wilson had been a respectable, law-abiding citizen all his life and he had associated with the same kind of people. His father had been a Presbyterian minister, and his mother was the daughter of another minister. As soon as Wilson got his degree of Doctor of Philosophy he went to teaching, and from that to the presidency of Princeton University. Naturally, such a man found it hard to be polite to someone he looked on as a thief and a murderer. Added to everything else, this Huerta was ignorant, foul-mouthed, drunk a large part of the time, and he kept around him people of the worst type. Everything about him set Wilson's teeth on edge.

Still, the fellow was in power in Mexico and had to be dealt with somehow. Wilson would have been wiser to move very carefully until the Mexicans themselves were thoroughly sick of Huerta. Instead, he announced that he would recognize no man as president of Mexico who got there by murdering the lawful president. One thing led to another, until Huerta's men arrested some American sailors who had been sent ashore at Tampico to get supplies. They were quickly released, with an apology, but the American admiral demanded in addition a formal salute to the American flag, which the Mexicans refused to give. News came that a German ship was bringing arms and ammunition to Huerta, and to stop it the American Navy bombarded and then seized the city of Vera Cruz.

You couldn't expect the Mexicans to like that, and they didn't. Several hundred of their men, as well as sixteen of ours, were killed in the attack, and even those who disliked Huerta said, "Better put up with him than be ruled by the United States." The Mexicans prepared for a war that they knew they could not win. War, though, was the last thing that Wilson wanted, so he was glad when Argentina, Brazil, and Chile, the ABC countries, offered to try to settle the quarrel.

The ABC countries suggested that both Huerta and the United States get out of Mexico and let the country be run by Victoriano Carranza, who had been a friend of Madero. This was agreed to, and we pulled out, looking rather foolish, but at least without fighting all Mexico. Carranza turned out to be a vain and stupid old fellow, without brains enough to govern a country like Mexico. Soon there were three armies fighting him — two under Orozco and Zapata in the south and in the north one army under a former cattle thief and bandit named Villa.

At first the United States carefully kept its hands off, but in 1916 Villa, having been defeated by one of Carranza's generals, thought he would create a diversion by attacking the United States. So he crossed the border, raided the town of Columbus, New Mexico, killed seventeen innocent people, and set fire to the town. This was too much. General John J. Pershing was ordered to go after Villa, into Mexico if necessary, and did so. Carranza objected violently to American soldiers on Mexican soil and, although he did not fire on them, hampered and harassed Pershing in every way he could. Villa was never captured. Carranza hung on for four years longer, but then he was defeated and murdered.

As things turned out, though, the bandit Villa may have done us a favor by showing us how weak our defenses were. Pershing discovered that the United States Army was in terrible shape. It was cut up into small detachments scattered all over the country, and it took a full month to get one division together on the border.

There wasn't enough of our Army to guard the whole Mexican border, so Wilson called out the

National Guard from many states. Some of them stayed there for months and they, as well as the regular army, did a great deal of drilling and marching and target practice, so that they were much better soldiers than they had been before.

Also Wilson discovered that Pershing was a very good soldier indeed. His job was a terrible one. He really had no chance to catch the fast-moving Villa, he had no proper equipment, the country through which he marched was largely waterless desert, and of course he was blamed for everything that went wrong, although little, if any of it, was his fault. Still, he never opened his mouth to criticize the President or the War Department; he simply went ahead and did his best.

By this time most Americans had forgotten Mexico in their excitement over the great war that we called at first the European War, and later the World War. (One of the saddest facts of history is that twenty years later we had to change the name again and call it World War I.)

In the summer of 1914 the excitement was so great that it is hard for us to imagine how it was. There had not been a really big war in Europe for more than forty years. Only a few old men were left of those who had been in the armies when France and Germany fought in 1870; and in this country the men who

had taken part in the Civil War were still older. Most of the world had no idea what a big war was like, and here was one coming that was plainly the biggest in all history — not merely two countries, but six, including five of the Great Powers, three on one side, three on the other. The Central Powers were Germany, Austria (strictly speaking, the Austro-Hungarian Empire), and Turkey. Against them were the Allies — Great Britain, France, and Russia. Japan and Italy were still hesitating, waiting for their chance to gain most at least cost.

Most Americans had a very dim idea of what the war was about. We knew that on June 28, 1914, a young Serbian had murdered the Archduke of Austria. We knew that the Austrian government said that the Serbian government had sent the assassin to commit the crime and the Serbian government said it hadn't, but Austria threatened to make war on Serbia anyhow. Then Russia offered to help Serbia, Germany got ready to help Austria, France to help Russia, and Great Britain to help France. Turkey came in to help Germany and Austria.

But still we were confused. Only people who remembered their geography knew that Serbia was a small kingdom, one of several in the Balkan mountains south of Austria. Many of us didn't know who the Archduke of Austria was. Even when we learned that he was a very important person, as important in Austria as the Prince of Wales in England, the Crown Prince in Germany, and the Czarevitch in Russia — that is, the heir to the throne — still he didn't seem important enough to justify a war involving all Europe.

Actually his murder was the excuse, not the real reason, for the war. The real reason was complicated and hard to understand. In fact, to know all about it, you would have to go to work and study the history of Europe during the hundred years since Napoleon, which few Americans had done. Woodrow Wilson was a historian and knew more about it than most of us, but even he was confused. After all, he had given most of his attention to the history of the United States, which had little to do with that of Europe.

But he was quite sure of one thing. This was that the United States was now a full-grown nation. It ought not to do anything in haste or in anger or merely because it liked one side and didn't like the other. Therefore he issued a proclamation saying that in the war this country was neutral: it was not for and was not against either side.

Most Americans agreed that was quite right. This country should keep its hands off, and let them fight it out among themselves. But Wilson's proclamation went further. It said, "We must be impartial in thought as well as in action, must put a curb upon our sentiments, as well as upon every transaction." That was asking too much, and many people felt the President had no right to ask it.

What Wilson meant, of course, was that we should not make up our minds until we had time to study all the facts; but that isn't what he said. He said, "We must be impartial in thought," and that was a mistake because it couldn't be done.

A great many Americans had come — or their fathers had come — from Germany and still loved the old country, so naturally they favored that side. Many more had come from Great Britain and favored the Allies. Then Italy, in spite of a treaty binding her to the Central Powers, broke away and joined the Allies, and the Italian-Americans, of whom there were millions, swung that way too. Finally, Japan joined the Allies and that made Americans who disliked Russia and Japan favor the Central Powers.

So there was a terrific uproar, British-Americans denouncing German-Americans and being denounced right back, Californians denouncing Japan, haters of tyrannical power denouncing Russia, pacifists denouncing both sides, and everybody denouncing Wilson. For Wilson was still convinced that the duty of America was first of all to keep cool, to study the facts, and to try to make an arrangement that would be fair to all sides and bring peace back to Europe.

It was a fine idea, but it wouldn't work. Within a very short time so much blood had been shed, and hatred had mounted so high in Europe that nothing less than an archangel could have made the fighting nations see reason, and Wilson was no angel. Indeed, the more he tried to convince Americans that they should keep cool, the more they suspected that he was more devil than angel. For instance, Theodore Roosevelt, who was strongly in favor of the Allies, suspected — and said loudly — that Wilson was really helping Germany. German-Americans were just as sure that he was helping the Allies.

In the meantime, battle after battle was proving that the fighters were about evenly matched, and both sides were growing desperate. So they became more and more careless of the rights of neutrals, including the United States. The British Navy was stronger than the German Navy in surface ships, but the Germans had more submarines, and began to use them against British merchantmen. Then the British mounted big guns on the merchantmen and thereafter the submarines did not dare come to the surface within range of those guns. So they simply torpedoed the ships without warning. Up to that time it had been the rule of civilized warfare that you could sink an enemy merchant ship, but first you had to take off all her people, which a submarine could not do. So when a German submarine sank a great British liner, the *Lusitania,* in 1915, drowning 1,198 people, of whom 124 were American passengers, this country was horrified and millions turned against Germany, even though British surface cruisers were constantly seizing American ships. The difference was that the British didn't drown anybody.

However, nobody wanted war. When the election of 1916 drew near and the Republicans nominated

Charles Evans Hughes, who was frankly in favor of the Allies, Wilson was re-elected, although by so narrow a margin that it took several days to find out who had won. After all, right or wrong, he had kept us out of war for two years and millions of Americans hoped that he could continue to keep us out.

But he knew, and he tried to tell the people, that the only way anybody could keep us out was to stop the war, and stop it very soon. He did everything he could think of to accomplish this, but by that time it was beyond the control of any man.

After the sinking of the *Lusitania*, Germany had promised not to do anything of that kind again and

had kept her word. But she was not winning the war and it looked less and less likely that she ever could win it on land. Her navy people, however, thought that she could win it on the sea by sinking every ship that approached the British Isles, neutral or not; and early in 1917 she announced that she was going to do it.

That almost forced Wilson to go to war then and there, because a furious outcry arose in this country. But still he waited, hoping that Germany would not do all that she threatened. Late in March, however, four American ships were sunk, one in the so-called safety zone off the Dutch coast. Then Wilson asked Congress to declare war against Germany.

He did this, not because he had changed his mind about the duty of America, but because he had decided that she could do her duty in no other way. He did not believe for a moment that all the right was on the Allied side and all the wrong on the German. He knew, for instance, that Russia under the czar was a tyranny, which had entered the war not to defend liberty but in the hope of getting Constantinople — the city once called Byzantium and now known as Istanbul. He knew that the French wanted to get back Alsace-Lorraine, an area that they had lost when they were beaten by Germany in 1870. He knew that the British wanted to cut down Germany before she got too strong to handle, because Germany was trying to build a bigger navy than Britain's and also because German merchants were taking a great deal of trade away from British merchants.

Wilson did not think that Americans should help in any of these projects. Still less did he think we should take advantage of the war to grab anything for ourselves, and he made that very clear in his message to Congress.

But aside from all these things, there was something much greater than all of them put together; and this thing, Wilson believed, swung the balance. The leaders of the German government had worked out, and the German people had accepted, a theory of government that was the exact opposite of the American theory, which was, to a large extent, also the British and French theory.

The German theory was that the state is in every way — not merely in some ways — greater than the man. Therefore the man's highest duty is to serve the state, and if he does not do it willingly he should be made to do it. One of Germany's greatest men said that the way to govern a great nation is by "blood and iron"; that is to say, by force.

Now Americans do not admit that the state is greater than the man in every way. Our theory is that men created the state, and created it in order that it might protect their rights, especially the three rights mentioned in the Declaration of Independence — life, liberty, and the pursuit of happiness.

Therefore it is our theory that the highest duty of the state is to serve the individual, not the other way about. Certainly a man must protect and defend the state, especially in time of war, but only in order that the state may protect and defend him in the enjoyment of his rights. If it fails in that, says the Declaration, "It is the right of the people to alter or abolish it." The state has no right to rule by "blood and iron," but only by convincing the people that it is doing what they created it for.

This is the theory that Washington fought for, that Jefferson worked out in detail, that Jackson applied, that Lincoln defended through four terrible years and that brought murder upon him in the end. This belief in liberty is what millions of Americans, who were not great and whose names are not remembered, have worked and fought and died for.

Slowly and sadly Woodrow Wilson came to believe what he had not believed at first; namely, that if the Central Powers won the war they would impose their theory on all Europe, and sooner or later on all the world. The idea that the state should be the servant of the man — the theory of liberty —

would disappear, and be replaced by the idea of the state as master of the man — the theory of blood and iron.

In that case, the duty of the United States was plain. It was to act as a mature nation should act, not guided by emotion but by cool reason, to throw its weight on the side whose victory seemed most likely "to secure the blessings of liberty to ourselves and our posterity."

On April 2, 1917, Woodrow Wilson, President of the United States, went before Congress and asked it to declare war against Germany. The man who spoke that day was not representing a small, weak people, a child nation struggling to be free. He was not speaking for a youthful nation, racked by pains and strains brought on by its own rapid growth. He spoke for a full-grown nation that was not seeking excitement or revenge or profit, but only to do its duty to itself and to the world, as a manful nation must always do. The President of grown-up America put it in these words:

"The world must be made safe for democracy. Its peace must be planted upon the tested foundations of political liberty. We have no selfish ends to serve. We desire no conquest, no dominion ... The day has come when America is privileged

to spend her blood and her might for the principles that gave her birth and happiness and the peace which she has treasured. God helping her, she can do no other."

Index

*Indicates illustrations

213

G

H